Blueprints 2

Blueprints 2

COMPOSITION SKILLS FOR ACADEMIC WRITING

Keith S. Folse
University of Central Florida

M. Kathleen Mahnke
Saint Michael's College

Elena Vestri Solomon
Teacher Trainer, UzTEA Uzbekistan

Lorraine Williams
Saint Michael's College

HEINLE
CENGAGE Learning™

Australia • Brazil • Japan • Korea • Mexico • Singapore • Spain • United Kingdom • United States

Blueprints 2: Composition Skills for Academic Writers
Keith S. Folse, M. Kathleen Mahnke, Elena Vestri Solomon, and Lorraine Williams

Editor in Chief: Patricia A. Coryell

Director of ESL Publishing: Susan Maguire

Senior Development Editor: Kathy Sands Boehmer

Editorial Assistant: Mira Bharin

Senior Project Editor: Kathryn Dinovo

Cover Design Manager: Diana Coe

Senior Manufacturing Coordinator: Jane Spelman

Marketing Manager: Annamarie Rice

Marketing Assistant: Sophie Xie

Production/Composition: Laurel Technical Services

Cover Image: © Ryan McVay/Getty Images/ PhotoDisc

Photo Credits: **p. 1:** © Eric Kamp/Index Stock Imagery. **p. 21:** © Bettmann/CORBIS. **p. 23 (top left):** © Bettmann/ CORBIS. **p. 23 (top right):** © Rufus F. Folkks/CORBIS. **p. 23 (bottom left):** © Darren Modricker/CORBIS. **p. 23 (bottom right):** © John Henley Photography/CORBIS. **p. 29:** © Lonnie Duka/ Index Stock Imagery. **p. 45:** © Richard T. Nowitz/CORBIS. **p. 46:** © Steve Kaufman/ CORBIS. **p. 57:** © Eric Kamp/Index Stock Imagery. **p. 84:** © Ryan McVay/Getty Images. **p. 93 (left):** © Corbis/SYGMA. **p. 93 (right):** © Corbis/ SYGMA. **p. 97 (left):** © Francie Manning/Index Stock Imagery. **p. 97 (right):** © Powerstock-ZEFA/Index Stock Imagery. **p. 117:** © Izzy Schwartz/Getty Images. **p. 145:** © Zephyr Pictures, Inc./ Index Stock Imagery. **p. 146:** © Adam Woolfitt/ CORBIS. **p. 149:** © Bettmann/CORBIS. **p. 152:** © Hulton-Deutsch Collection/CORBIS. **p. 159:** ©Hartmut Schwarzbach/UNEP/ Still Pictures. **p. 160:** © Craig Orsini/Index Stock Imagery. **p. 166:** © Paul Hutley; Eye Ubiquitous/CORBIS. **p. 186:** © Stewart Cohen/Index Stock Imagery. **p. 191:** © Chuck Savage/CORBIS. **p. 200:** © Ryan McVay/Getty Images.

Library of Congress Control Number: 2001131497

ISBN-13: 978-0-618-14410-5

ISBN-10: 0-618-14410-2

Heinle
20 Channel Center Street
Boston, MA 02210
USA

Cengage Learning is a leading provider of customized learning solutions with office locations around the globe, including Singapore, the United Kingdom, Australia, Mexico, Brazil, and Japan. Locate your local office at **www.cengage.com/global**

Cengage Learning products are represented in Canada by Nelson Education, Ltd.

Visit Heinle online at **elt.heinle.com**

Visit our corporate website at **www.cengage.com**

Printed in the United States of America
19 20 21 22 21 20 19 18

CONTENTS

Unit 2

CLASSIFICATION ESSAYS 29

Unit 3

PROCESS ESSAYS 57

BLUEPRINTS 2 SKILLS CHART (PART A)

Unit	Blueprint Topics	Coherence Devices/ Transition Expressions	Grammar Focus and Sentence Check	Skills Practice
1 Paragraph to Essay	The Paragraph Unity and Coherence in Paragraphs The Essay The Thesis Statement Essay Introductions The Body of the Essay Essay Conclusions			Reviewing paragraph structure Working with essay introductions, bodies, and conclusions Incorporating unity and coherence in writing
2 Classification Essays	What Is a Classification Essay? Unity in Classification Essays Coherence in Classification Essays	*one/another/a third (fourth, etc.)* + classifying word	Passive voice Adjective clauses	Determining principles of classification Classifying information Maintaining unity and coherence in classification essays
3 Process Essays	What is a Process Essay? Types of Process Essays Introductions in Process Essays Conclusions in Process Essays Unity in Process Essays Coherence in Process Essays	*first (second, third, etc.), next, now, then, finally,* *before, after, once,* *as soon as, while* + sentence; *during, over, between* + noun phrase	Articles Adverb clauses	Understanding analytical and informational processess Thinking about your audience Explaining a process Maintaining unity and coherence in process essays
4 Comparison/ Contrast Essays	What is a Comparison/ Contrast Essay? Three Oraganizational Methods of Comparison/Contrast Unity in Comparison/ Contrast Essays Coherence inComparison/ Contrast Essays	*both* noun *and* noun, *not only . . . but also . . .,* *nevertheless, on one hand . . . on the other hand, in contrast,* *whereas, unlike* + noun, *like* + noun, *conversely, although,* *even though, though*	Comparisons Parallelism	Working with different methods of organization for comparison/ contrast Maintaining unity and coherence in comparison/ contrast essays

BLUEPRINTS 2 SKILLS CHART (PART A CONTINUED)

Unit	Blueprint Topics	Coherence Devices/ Transition Expressions	Grammar Focus and Sentence Check	Skills Practice
5 Cause/Effect Essays	What is a Cause/Effect Essay? Methods of Organization for Cause/Effect Essays Unity in Cause/Effect Essays Coherence in Cause/Effect Essays	*because/as/since* + s + v, *therefore, consequently, thus, as a result* + s + v, *as a result of*	Verb tense review Fragments, run-ons, and comma splices	Working with different methods of cause/effect organization Maintaining unity and coherence in cause/effect essays
6 Reaction Essays	What is a Reaction Essay? Unity in Reaction Essays Coherence in Reaction Essays	Repeating key terms or phrases Using pronouns Using synonyms	Word forms Sentence variety	Practicing reactions Maintaining unity and coherence in reaction essays
7 Argumentative Essays	What Is an Argumentative Essay? Developing and Supporting an Argument Understanding Both Sides Maintaining a Stance Introductions in Argumentative Essays Methods of Organization for Argumentative Essays Unity in Argumentative Essays Coherence in Argumentative Essays	*although it may be true that,* *despite the fact that, certainly, surely*	Prepositions Noun clauses	Determining the opposing sides of an argument Working with different methods of organizing arguments Supporting arguments with details Maintaining unity and coherence in argumentative essays

BLUEPRINTS 2 SKILLS CHART (PART B) *THE WRITING PROCESS*

Unit	Prewriting	Planning	Writing	Additional Writing Assignments from the Academic Disciplines
1 Paragraph to Essay	Brainstorming	Outlining Giving and receiving feedback on outlines	Writing an essay Giving and receiving feedback on first draft Editing and revising Completing final draft	– Business – Science – Technology – Literature
2 Classification Essays	Using a questionnaire	Using a tree diagram Giving and receiving feedback on tree diagrams	Writing a classification essay, using "posing a question" as an introductory technique Giving and receiving feedback on first draft Editing and revising Completing final draft	– Business – Science – Technology – Social Science – Linguistics
3 Process Essays	Visualizing Sketching Listing	Using a flow chart Giving and receiving feedback on flowcharts	Writing a process essay, using the "funnel method" as an introductory technique Giving and receiving feedback on first draft Editing and revising	– Business – Science – Anthropology – Psychology
4 Comparison/ Contrast Essays	Listing	Using a T-diagram Giving and receiving feedback on T-diagrams	Writing a comparison/contrast essay, using "quotation" as an introductory hook Giving and receiving feedback on first draft Editing and revising Completing final draft	– Business – Science – History – Linguistics – Travel

BLUEPRINTS 2 SKILLS CHART (PART B CONTINUED) *THE WRITING PROCESS*

Unit	Prewriting	Planning	Writing	Additional Writing Assignments from the Academic Disciplines
5 Cause/Effect Essays	Using a spoke diagram	Using a chart Giving and receiving feedback on charts	Writing a cause/effect essay, using a "dramatic statement" as an introductory technique Giving and receiving feedback on first draft Editing and revising Completing final draft	– Business – Science – Technology – Geology – Current Issues
6 Reaction Essays	Using your eyes as "a camera"	Combining reactions and descriptions in a chart Giving and receiving feedback on charts	Writing a reaction essay, giving background information in the introduction Giving and receiving feedback on first draft Editing and revising Completing final draft	– Entertainment – Politics – Literature – Lecture Analysis
7 Argumentative Essays	Searching for sources of information to support your argument	Synthesizing information from outside sources Outlining	Writing an argumentative essay, using "turning an argument on its head" as an introductory technique Giving and receiving feedback on first draft Editing and revising Completing final draft	– Business – Science – Sociology/Political – Science – Linguistics

Unit 8

This section includes special instruction and practice in the important academic writing skills of paraphrasing, summarizing, and synthesizing information.

WELCOME TO BLUEPRINTS!

Blueprints 2: Composition Skills for Academic Writing is the second in a two-volume writing series for students of English as a second language. *Blueprints 2* is designed for students at the high-intermediate and advanced levels. *Blueprints 1* is designed for intermediate-level students. Both books are aimed at preparing students for success in academic writing. *Blueprints 1* focuses primarily on the paragraph, with a final unit devoted to the essay. *Blueprints 2* moves students from the paragraph to the essay in its first unit and focuses on the essay from that point on. Each *Blueprints* text features direct instruction in academic composition skills, short reading passages that serve as blueprints for writing tasks, presentations of key ESL grammar points, a large number of practice exercises, and a variety of real writing assignments.

TO THE TEACHER

Series Approach

Recent research in ESL writing instruction points to the inextricable link between the two skills of reading and writing. The *Blueprints* series builds upon this connection by using reading to support the instruction of writing. For example, students using *Blueprints* practice reading for main ideas, details, and so forth, before practicing these features in their writing. In addition, in both *Blueprints 1* and *Blueprints 2,* students read and analyze numerous **"blueprint" model paragraphs and essays** that exemplify the rhetorical modes and other techniques of writing they are learning. **Connections between reading and writing** are exploited throughout both texts to the maximum benefit of students.

Over the past several years, research and practice in the teaching of ESL writing have also established both the writing process and the written product as important instructional focuses. With this in mind, another key component of the *Blueprints* approach is the incorporation of writing **process/product practice.** In each unit, a writing topic is assigned and students follow a series of process steps, from prewriting through peer and teacher review of various drafts to a final, finished product. This portion of each unit incorporates the most current philosophies regarding the importance of the writing process, from audience response and feedback to the creation of a final written product.

In order to facilitate **peer review** of writing, **partner feedback forms** are provided for each writing assignment. These response forms are designed to be written on directly. However, some teachers prefer having students write directly on one another's papers, using the questions on the partner feedback forms to guide them. Others find that the partner feedback forms are most effective as catalysts for paired discussions rather than as mechanisms for formal response. A variety of possibilities exist for using *Blueprints* partner feedback forms, and we encourage teachers to experiment with them.

Both volumes 1 and 2 of *Blueprints* provide instruction in the **rhetorical modes** that comprise the bulk of academic writing across the disciplines. Additionally, the texts help students work on **topic** and **thesis statements, introductions, body sentences** and **paragraphs,** and **conclusions.** *Blueprints 2* also provides beginning instruction in **research skills.** As detailed instruction in these skills is not within the scope of the *Blueprints* series, we recommend that teachers who want to do further work with their students in this area have students use a research and writing handbook alongside *Blueprints.*

A unique feature of the *Blueprints* series is the addition of three important yet often neglected aspects of academic writing, namely **paraphrasing, summarizing,** and **synthesizing** information from more than one source. Other composition topics that are treated include reaction paper writing as well as special attention to techniques for assuring coherence and unity in writing. In particular, the practices involving paraphrasing, summarizing, and synthesizing represent an innovative way for learners to hone their abilities with these extremely important composition skills.

Another important feature of the *Blueprints* series approach is its attention to **grammar instruction and practice.** Both ESL teachers and ESL students recognize the fact that grammar surfaces as a particularly challenging element of second language writing. With this in mind, grammar points that are particularly useful to writers at the intermediate and advanced levels are explained, exemplified in the model readings, and practiced in each unit of both *Blueprints* books.

About the Books

Each *Blueprints* text begins with an introductory unit. In *Blueprints 1,* this unit presents the paragraph as well as the skills of paraphrasing, summarizing, and synthesizing. In its first unit, *Blueprints 2* reviews the paragraph and introduces the essay, as well as various techniques for writing introductions and conclusions, and the concepts of unity and coherence. The remaining units in each book are organized around rhetorical modes, with special attention given to other selected aspects of academic writing. (See individual tables of contents for details.)

Each unit in the *Blueprints* texts is divided into two parts. Part A is the instructional portion. Part B leads the student through the steps of the writing process as it applies to the rhetorical mode introduced in the unit. Each part begins with a clearly stated list of objectives so that teachers and students alike can determine the relevance of these objectives to real student needs.

TO THE STUDENT

Without a doubt, good writing requires many skills. Good writing requires your ability to use words and sentences correctly, and very good writing requires the ability to organize these words and sentences into paragraphs and essays that readers can understand well. Good writing means mastery of basic punctuation, capitalization, and spelling rules. In addition, good writing includes a solid grasp of English sentence structure, or grammar, to express ideas in writing that is accurate and appropriate.

Good writing in an academic setting often requires you to take information from one or more sources to produce a piece of writing that satisfies a certain writing task. Common examples of these academic writing tasks include summarizing a story, reacting to a piece of writing, and combining information into a new paragraph or essay.

Blueprints prepares you to be a good academic writer. One of the primary goals of the *Blueprints* books is to help you move beyond writing simple paragraphs and essays that are based on general or personal information to writing paragraphs and essays that are based on academic-level readings. The tasks in these books mirror what you will have to do in your college-level courses.

The following chart lists some special features of the *Blueprints* texts and their benefits to you.

FEATURE	BENEFIT
Blueprint readings exemplifying writing	The readings provide examples of good writing.
Grammar instruction and practice	The grammar instruction and practice help student writers master grammar in their writing.
Paraphrasing, summarizing, and synthesizing practice	These three specific skills may be the best help students will ever find for composition.
Academic writing assignments at the end of each unit	Student writing can actually reflect their learning goals.

PREFACE TO BLUEPRINTS 2

Text Organization

Blueprints 2 is divided into eight units. Unit 1 reviews the elements of a good paragraph and introduces the essay. It also introduces strategies for maintaining unity and coherence in academic writing and provides students with a variety of techniques for writing effective introductions. Concepts introduced in Unit 1 are recycled and further developed in subsequent units. Unity and coherence, for example, are revisited in each successive unit, and each successive unit also focuses on one of the introductory techniques introduced in Unit 1. Units 2 through 7 practice different kinds of essays. Unit 8 differs somewhat in format from the other units. It treats the important academic writing skills of paraphrasing, summarizing, and synthesizing.

This book is organized with a rhetorical mode as the primary vehicle for practicing organized composition. Unit 2 practices classification essays, perhaps the most straightforward of the essay types. Unit 3 focuses on process essays. Unit 4 features comparison/contrast essays. Unit 5 provides practice in cause/effect essays, and Unit 6 introduces the reaction essay. Unit 7 provides instruction and practice in the argumentative essay, one of the most common, yet most complex, essay types used in academic writing. These rhetorical modes were chosen because surveys of college and university programs cited them as those most often taught in freshman writing programs.

Contents of a Unit

Part A

Composition Lesson

Each unit begins with the core material for the unit, consisting of a presentation of the rhetorical mode for that unit. This presentation is followed by a series of short exercises that provide step-by-step practice with the unit's writing lesson.

Readings

Because of the important link between reading and writing, every unit contains two *Blueprints* reading passages (150–250 words) that students work with before they attempt any original writing. Each reading passage is designed to be a model of the rhetorical mode being taught. Each also models an introductory technique that students will practice later. All readings are preceded by a brief set of questions to help activate the schema necessary for ultimate reading comprehension. Along with each reading passage are glossed key vocabulary as well as questions that require students to analyze not only the content of the passage but also various composition elements that are featured in the reading passage. The focus on vocabulary is extremely important because a more solid grasp of lexical items will help students move from basic writing to more advanced writing. Likewise, the focus on composition elements provides not only focused instruction but also sufficient guided practice.

Grammar Focus and Sentence Check

Because grammar is such an integral part of any good writing, there are two kinds of grammar presentations in each unit: discrete grammar and sentence-level grammar. The points practiced in these two categories vary from unit to unit and are designed to address grammar that is particularly challenging for ESL writers.

Part B

Writing Assignment

Students are given a specific writing assignment that is based on the rhetorical mode presented in the unit. In Unit 4, for example, students write an original comparison/contrast essay. With all students working on the same assignment, the writing instructor has an opportunity to teach the whole group. At any point during the writing process, the teacher and class can address areas of concern.

Prewriting

Each unit presents some type of prewriting activity. This particular activity varies from unit to unit.

Planning

After generating ideas, students use a planning device or technique to organize them. Once again the details of this activity vary from unit to unit.

Partner Feedback 1

After the planning process, students are encouraged to give one another feedback. Feedback at this stage helps to identify areas that students should attend to before attempting a first draft.

First draft

As students write their first draft, they can use the special checklists for writing introductions, bodies, and conclusions that can help them produce unified and coherent essays.

Partner Feedback 2

Feedback is again encouraged after the first draft. As many academic classes require group work, repeated practice with a familiar and sympathetic ESL audience is helpful in a general way. In addition, group/pair work also allows students to exchange ideas about a given topic. Finally, group/pair work can be valuable because other student readers tend to be more critical than the writer and therefore more likely to find errors than students usually do in self-editing.

Final Draft

At this point, students are asked to revise their work again, using the feedback they received from their peers and teachers. Another checklist is provided to guide them in reviewing their work one final time.

Additional Writing Assignments from the Academic Disciplines

A unique feature of this book is a chart found at the end of every unit. This chart features a list of four to six academic areas, each with a writing prompt for a topic. The writing prompts lend themselves well to the rhetorical mode being presented and practiced in that particular unit.

Appendices

In addition to the appendix for Partner Feedback Forms, *Blueprints 2* provides appendices on Paragraph Practice, Guidelines for Partner Feedback, Creating Essay Titles, and Finding and Documenting Information from Sources.

Answer Key

The Answer Key for *Blueprints 2* is available on the Heinle website: elt.heinle.com/blueprints

Instructor's Notes and Extra Exercises

Helpful notes for instructors using *Blueprints 2* as well as extra exercises for students are also available at elt.heinle.com/blueprints.

ACKNOWLEDGMENTS

This book and its companion text *Blueprints 1* are the result of L2 writing, research, and discussion as well as L2 teaching experience and learning experience with writing. We would like to thank those educators and learners who helped us arrive at our current understanding of L2 writing by sharing their insights, teaching ideas, and learning hints.

The four of us offer a very special word of thanks to our editors who have been so great throughout the development of the *Blueprints* books. Huge thanks go to Susan Maguire, who has been a constant source of guidance and inspiration from the very inception of this series. Likewise, we are tremendously indebted to Kathy Sands Boehmer, who provided just the right amounts of positive feedback and gentle nudging throughout the completion of this project. In addition, we are forever grateful to our developmental editor, Kathleen Smith, whose careful editing and diligent work have played an integral role in the creation of this final product.

We would also like to thank the following reviewers who offered ideas and suggestions that shaped our revisions: Prof. Jim Bame, Utah State University; Carolyn Baughan, Illinois State University; Jane Curtis, Roosevelt University; Judy W. Davis, Oklahoma State University; Zeljana Grubisic, University of Maryland at Baltimore County; Jody Hacker, Missions College; Daryl Kinney, Los Angeles City College; Manuel Munoz; Michael Roehm, American University; Anne-Marie Schlender, Austin Community College.

Keith S. Folse
M. Kathleen Mahnke
Elena Vestri Solomon
Lorraine Williams

UNIT 1

Blueprints for

PARAGRAPH TO ESSAY

PART A

Blueprints for the Paragraph and the Essay

Objectives	In Part A, you will:
Analysis:	review the three basic parts of a paragraph
	identify and analyze the three basic parts of an essay
	learn about and analyze thesis statements
	learn techniques for writing effective essay introductions, bodies, and conclusions
Unity and Coherence:	learn about unity and coherence in paragraphs and essays
Practice:	practice working with essay introductions, bodies, and conclusions
	practice unity and coherence in writing

The Paragraph

One of the basic building blocks of academic writing is the **paragraph.** A paragraph is a group of sentences that work together to develop one main idea. The main idea is often stated in the first sentence of the paragraph, **the topic sentence.** The topic sentence includes the topic and a **controlling idea,** which gives a focus to the topic and often gives the reader information about the organization of the paragraph. After the topic sentence comes the **body.** Sentences in the body of the paragraph support or develop the main idea in the topic sentence. Most paragraphs end with a **concluding sentence.** This sentence either summarizes the ideas in the paragraph or acts as a transition to the next paragraph.

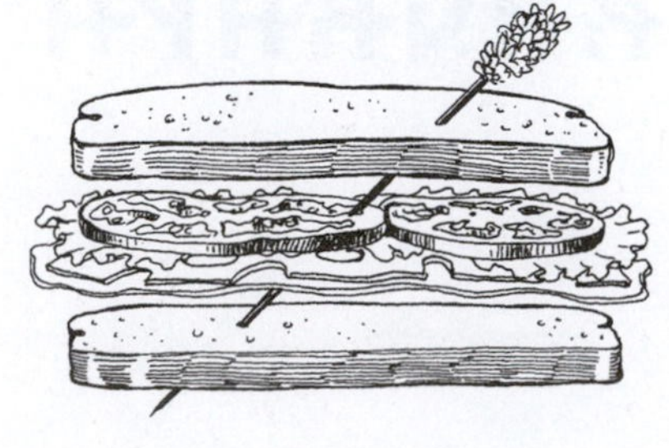

EXERCISE 1

The Three Parts of the Paragraph

Read the paragraph and answer the questions.

Writing for a Purpose

Paragraphs and essays are often categorized according to their purposes. One purpose is to explain a process. Writers use a process paragraph or essay to tell how to do something, for example, how to change a tire. Another purpose is to classify, and writers use classification paragraphs and essays to categorize things, for example, different kinds of insects or cars. A third purpose is to compare and contrast. Writers compare and contrast when they write about such things as choosing among jobs, movies, or investment strategies. Yet another purpose is to show cause and effect. Cause/effect paragraphs and essays analyze why things happen the way they do. A final and important purpose for writing is to give an opinion or argue a point of view. This purpose is the basis for much academic writing. Categorizing paragraphs and essays according to their purposes is a convenient and useful way of describing them.

1. Write the paragraph's topic sentence here. Circle the topic and underline the controlling idea.

   ____

   ____

2. Write one sentence here from the body of the paragraph.

   ____

   ____

   Does it support or develop the main idea in the topic sentence?

   ____

3. Write the paragraph's concluding sentence here.

   ____

   ____

   Does the concluding sentence summarize or relate to the topic sentence?

   ____

4. What is the primary purpose of this paragraph? (Circle one.)
   a. To explain a process
   b. To classify
   c. To state an opinion
   d. To discuss cause and effect

5. How many kinds of paragraphs are discussed in this paragraph?

____

List them here.

____

____

____

____

Unity and Coherence in Paragraphs

Unity and coherence are essential components of a good paragraph. They help your writing make sense and flow smoothly.

Unity

One characteristic of good writing is **unity.** Each paragraph you write, whether it stands alone or is part of a longer essay, should have unity. When a paragraph has unity, all of the sentences in it relate to the topic and develop the controlling idea. If a topic sentence states that a paragraph will be about how to prepare for a successful job interview, all sentences in the paragraph should talk about job interview preparation. Adding sentences about how to talk to your new boss once you are hired would destroy the paragraph's unity. Unity is important in all types of writing. In each unit in Blueprints 2, you will study techniques for planning and writing paragraphs and essays with unity.

EXERCISE

Paragraph Unity

Read each topic sentence. Draw a line through the sentence that does not support this topic sentence. On the blank line, explain your choice. The first one is done for you.

1. Topic sentence: The crow is a large black bird with some surprising characteristics.
   a. Many crows actually seem to enjoy being with people.
   b. Crows like to spend time communicating with one another and sometimes seem to have long and involved conversations.
   ~~c. The raven is a relative of the crow, but the two are very different.~~
   d. Crows also seem to feel sympathy when they see other injured birds.

   Explanation: *I chose C because it talks about ravens, but the topic of the paragraph is not ravens. It's crows.*

2. Topic sentence: Life in the interior of Alaska is quite challenging in the winter.
   a. In the summer, the temperature outdoors averages a perfect 70 degrees Fahrenheit.
   b. For most of the winter, interior roads are closed to all vehicles except snowmobiles.
   c. Temperatures regularly dip to 40 or 50 degrees Fahrenheit below zero, making it impossible to go outside without special clothing.
   d. Fresh fruits and vegetables are unavailable in the winter, even for a premium price, so maintaining a balanced diet is a challenge.

   Explanation: ____

   ____

3. Topic sentence: To answer questions about the past, historians use different kinds of evidence.
   a. They examine primary sources, or firsthand written accounts of people who lived in the past.
   b. They use unwritten evidence—carvings, statues, ancient ruins, and the like—to piece together historical information.
   c. In the face of evidence, historians must determine what is accurate and what is false or biased.
   d. Historians also gather information from secondary sources, or accounts that have already been written about the historical events.

   Explanation: ____

   ____

Coherence

Another important characteristic of good writing is **coherence.** Coherent writing flows smoothly and ideas are arranged logically. There are many different ways to make your writing coherent.

Strategies for Coherence

1. Make sure you arrange your ideas in a logical order. Sometimes this will be chronological order. (See Unit 3, pp. 57–83.)

   Example:

Incorrect: There are several steps involved in baking an angel food cake. After you sift the flour, add the sugar to it. First, sift the flour.

Correct: There are several steps involved in baking an angel food cake. First, sift the flour. Then add the sugar to it.

2. Repeat key words, use appropriate pronouns, and use synonyms. (See Unit 6, pp. 147–149.)

Example:

I saw a very interesting **man** at **the supermarket** yesterday. **The supermarket** (repetition of key word) was a busy place, and everyone seemed to be in a hurry, except for **this customer** (synonym). There **he** (appropriate pronoun) stood, with a line of people behind him, blocking the produce aisle, gazing at the eggplants.

Transition Expressions

Use transition expressions to link your ideas together smoothly. Units 2, 3, 4, 5, and 7 each feature different transition expressions appropriate to that unit's essay type. Here is a small sampling:

Unit 3: You should put the egg in the water **first. Next,** heat the water until it boils.

Unit 5: A practice that has been around for almost three thousand years will certainly not disappear any time soon. **In fact,** the number of plastic surgery operations performed is growing steadily. **However,** before turning to the knife to alter physical appearance, it is important to ask the simple question, "Why?"

Unit 7: **Although it may be true** that there appear to be dry riverbeds on the planet Mars, this does not prove that water or life once existed there.

EXERCISE 3

Arranging Ideas in Logical Order

In the following paragraph, the topic sentence and the concluding sentence are in the correct place. However, one or more of the supporting sentences is out of order. Make the paragraph coherent by rearranging the supporting sentences in the correct order.

Coal Formation

Topic Sentence: The coal we burn as fuel today began long ago as trees and other plants that grew beside water. (1) Movement of the rocks underneath then crushed some of the brown lignite coal even more and heated it, forming a hard black coal called *anthracite*. (2) Instead, they piled up, gradually forming a soft brown substance called *peat,* which was eventually buried. (3) When these plants died and fell to earth, they could not rot completely because the ground was too wet. (4) The peat was then crushed by its own weight and the weight of the rocks above it,

(continued)

(continued)

making it harder and turning it into *lignite,* or *brown coal.* **Concluding sentence:** This process of coal formation from living plants took place very slowly over millions of years.

Adapted from N. Curtis, M. Allaby, *Planet Earth* (New York: Kingfisher Books, 1993) p. 74.

EXERCISE 4

Repeating Key Words and Synonyms; Using Appropriate Pronouns

Read the paragraph. Underline the key words and synonyms in the topic sentence and throughout the paragraph. Correct any incorrect use of pronouns.

An Amazing Animal

On the way back to our hotel one night during our vacation on the beautiful island of Tasmania, my husband and I encountered a very strange animal. This animal had four legs and a furry body. At first they thought it was a beaver, because we also had a long flat tail. Then, however, we noticed something odd about its head. Instead of a beaver's mouth, you had a bill, like that of a duck or some other bird. What a strange thing! When we got back to our room, we asked the desk clerk for information about this peculiar beast because we both thought you were seeing things! We were relieved to find out that a furry mammal with a duck-like bill is not just a figment of their imagination. Strange as it may seem, such an animal actually does exist. Do you know what she is?

EXERCISE 5

Using Transition Words

Circle the word or phrase that joins each pair of ideas coherently.

1. Angela loves chocolate; (however/for example), she really doesn't like ice cream.
2. (During/while) the movie, our power went out.
3. (Although/Not only) the West Nile virus has shown up in New York City, doctors are not too worried that it might move to other parts of New York.
4. In the last decade, much progress was made in the area of AIDS research; (nevertheless/in addition), there is still no cure for this deadly disease.
5. Hawaii has a moderate climate; (consequently/as), it never gets excessively hot or cold there.

NOTE: **You can stop here and practice paragraph writing before continuing on to the essay. See Appendix 1, p. 217, for paragraph writing topics and a checklist to guide you.**

The Essay

Most academic writing is longer than one paragraph. In fact, paragraphs are usually building blocks for **essays.** An **essay** is a group of paragraphs about one topic. Like a good paragraph, a good essay is unified and coherent. You can use the same techniques in both to achieve unity and coherence. You can classify essays and paragraphs according to the same purposes (process, cause/effect, etc.), but an essay contains more details and examples than a paragraph. Therefore, it is a larger piece of writing.

Each essay has three major parts: **an introduction, a body,** and **a conclusion.** These parts correspond to the three major parts of the paragraph, but they are longer. An essay's introductory paragraph contains some general statements about the essay topic as well as its **thesis statement.** The thesis statement, like a paragraph's topic sentence, gives focus to the essay, presents the controlling ideas of the essay, and provides information about the organization of the essay.

IMPORTANT NOTE:

Essays can be as short as three paragraphs or as long as 20 or 30 paragraphs. A common length for essays in college writing is four to seven paragraphs.

Each paragraph in the body of an essay supports the thesis statement. Each contains a topic sentence and supporting sentences that are linked together coherently and that develop the essay topic. The essay's conclusion, like the paragraph's concluding sentence, summarizes the essay's main ideas and brings it to an end.

EXERCISE 

From Paragraph to Essay

A. *Read the paragraph and answer the question.*

Job Skills

One way in which career counselors classify jobs is according to the broadly-defined categories of the skills that the jobs require. Counselors like to try to match these categories with areas of strength for those who seek the job. Counselors today consider three major skill categories: interpersonal skills, mental skills, and physical skills. Interpersonal skills help us establish and maintain personal relationships. We put them to use when we communicate with others, either in person or by other means. Mental skills are the skills of the mind. We use these skills when we process information, come up with and think through ideas, and plan how to transform ideas into actions. We rely on our physical skills when we use our hands or bodies. These are the skills that we need when we engage in the variety of physical activities that occur in our working lives. According to today's career counselors, it is important to think about our strengths in all three of these skill areas when we are trying to find a career that fits our needs.

The three categories of skills in this paragraph support the controlling idea, but they provide limited information. What kinds of details could the writer add to expand each category and make it more clear for the reader? Jot down some of your ideas here.

interpersonal skills: ______________________________

____

mental skills: ______________________________

____

physical skills: ______________________________

____

B. *Read the essay, which is an expanded version of the paragraph in part A. Then answer the questions.*

sifting through: examining carefully

Job Skills

Are you looking for a job? How do you go about **sifting through** the seemingly endless stream of information available to find that one job for you? Well, career counselors, who are trained to help people find their ideal jobs, can be very helpful in your job search. One way in which career counselors try to match people with their ideal jobs is according to the broadly-defined categories of skills that the jobs require. Counselors today consider three major skill categories: interpersonal skills, mental skills, and physical skills.

Interpersonal skills help us establish and maintain personal relationships. We put them to use when we communicate with others, either in person or by other means. For example, people who work in retail sales, real estate, or other merchandising areas need highly developed interpersonal skills. Interpersonal skills are also very important for people in the so-called "helping" professions—doctors, nurses, teachers, and social workers. In fact, today's medical schools are giving almost as much weight to the interpersonal skills of their applicants as they do to their mental skills when evaluating these candidates for acceptance into their training programs.

Mental skills are the skills of the mind. We use these skills when we process information, come up with and think through ideas, and plan how to transform ideas into actions. Mental skills are obviously important for writers, academics, and researchers. But these are not the only careers that demand high-level mental skills. Any job that involves helping people solve problems—from what color hat to choose to how to cope with

(continued)

insomnia: inability to sleep

stamina: endurance

dexterity: skill in physical movement, especially of the hands

(continued)

stress, depression, or **insomnia**—demands mental skills. These skills include such general abilities as synthesizing, analyzing, perceiving, and visualizing and are thus important in many fields.

We rely on our physical skills when we use our bodies. These are the skills that we need when we engage in the variety of physical activities that occur in our working lives. Physical skills involve such things as **stamina, dexterity,** and physical strength. These skills are especially important for people who spend their time moving, carrying, and lifting things. Athletes, mail carriers, truck drivers, farmers, ranchers, and others who work outdoors often must rely heavily on their physical skills.

Few jobs involve only one of the three major skill types; most jobs need all of them, at least to a certain extent. Even a computer programmer, who may sit for hours at a time in front of her computer, needs a key physical skill. Without finger dexterity, her job would be quite challenging! However, most jobs do require greater competence in one of the three skill areas than they do in the others. According to today's career counselors, it is important to think about our strengths in all three of these skill areas when we are trying to find a career that fits our needs.

1. Find the thesis statement of this essay and write it here.

____

____

____

2. Underline the topic sentence in each supporting paragraph.
3. How are the skill categories introduced in part A expanded upon and supported in the essay?
   a. by telling a story
   b. by giving examples and explaining them
   c. by introducing more major categories
   d. by describing the steps in a process
4. Does the author use any of the ideas you suggested in part A to expand this paragraph into an essay? If so, which ones?

____

____

____

EXERCISE
7

From Paragraph to Essay

Look again at the paragraph and the essay in Exercise 6. Write the sentences from the paragraph on the appropriate lines in the essay diagram below to illustrate the ways in which a paragraph can be expanded into an essay. Draw lines from the paragraph sentences to the diagram.

PARAGRAPH

Job Skills

One way in which career counselors classify jobs is according to the broadly-defined categories of the skills that the jobs require. Counselors like to try to match these categories with areas of strength for those who seek the job. Counselors today consider three major skill categories: interpersonal skills, mental skills, and physical skills. Interpersonal skills help us establish and maintain personal relationships. We put them to use when we communicate with others, either in person or by other means. Mental skills are the skills of the mind. We use these skills when we process information, come up with and think through ideas, and plan how to transform ideas into actions. We rely on our physical skills when we use our hands or bodies. These are the skills that we need when we engage in the variety of physical activities that occur in our working lives. According to today's career counselors, it is important to think about our strengths in all three of these skill areas when we are trying to find a career that fits our needs.

ESSAY

Introduction

Thesis Statement: ______________________

____

____

Body Paragraph 1

Topic Sentence: ______________________

____

____

Body Paragraph 2

Topic Sentence: ______________________

____

____

Body Paragraph 3

Topic Sentence: ______________________

____

____

Conclusion

Concluding Sentence: ______________________

____

____

The Thesis Statement

The **thesis statement** of an essay is similar in purpose to the topic sentence of a paragraph. It presents the topic and the controlling idea for the entire essay. The thesis statement also often acts as a guide to other important information:

- the purpose and corresponding organizational structure of the essay
- the writer's point of view or opinion about the topic

IMPORTANT NOTE:

The thesis statement is the "key" to the essay. Without this key it is difficult to unlock the meaning of the essay.

Some thesis statements mention the subdivisions or subtopics that will be treated in the essay. Each of these subtopics then becomes a separate paragraph in the body of the essay. Other thesis statements do not provide the subtopics, but they indirectly say what they will be.

Direct Thesis Statement: The financial problems that small residential liberal arts colleges face are the direct result of a decrease in the number of college-age students nationwide, an increase in the proportion of those students who prefer technical and professional training over the traditional liberal arts, and the rapid and far-reaching effects of the distance education movement.

Indirect Thesis Statement: There are a number of causes for the financial problems that small residential liberal arts colleges face.

EXERCISE

Thesis Statements

Read the thesis statements and answer the questions.

1. Four major components make up the marketing mix of any successful business: the product itself, the product price, the means of product distribution, and the means of product promotion.

   a. What is the topic of this essay? marketing succesful business

   b. What subtopics will be discussed? The product itself .... 4 suptopics

   c. Is this a direct or an indirect thesis statement? Direct T.S.

   d. How many paragraphs will there probably be in the body of this essay? 4

e. Does the writer express an opinion in this thesis statement?

____

If so, what is it? ________________________

____

2. Depression strikes an increasing number of people each year, and its effects can be devastating.

a. What is the topic of this essay? Depression

____

b. Is this a direct or an indirect thesis statement? indirect

____

c. What is the purpose of this essay? ________________________

____

3. You only have to scratch the surface to see how damaging competitive sports really are to the overall psychological development of children.

a. What is the topic of this essay? ________________________

____

b. Is this a direct or an indirect thesis statement? ____________

____

c. Does the author express an opinion in this thesis statement?

____

If so, what is it? ________________________

____

Essay Introductions

The **introduction** is what readers read first, so it is very important. The introduction presents the essay topic in general. In addition, through the thesis statement, the introduction guides the reader to the essay's overall organization and purpose. The introduction should also include a "hook," something that grabs readers' attention and makes them want to read further.

Techniques for Writing Essay Introductions

You can use many techniques for writing introductions. The ones described here are hooks to engage readers. You will practice them in later units.

1. **Posing an interesting or controversial question or questions.** (practiced in Unit 2) This technique works well as a hook to draw the reader into the essay. After writers pose the questions, they give general ideas and background information and, finally, the thesis statement.

Example:

What if you were to wake up tomorrow morning and have no memory of the past? How would you function? Would you even know who you were? As unlikely as this may seem, it is not impossible. More and more Americans are finding themselves suffering from memory loss, some of it quite fast and without warning. Although one contributor to memory loss is Alzheimer's disease, there are other major causes as well, which can be classified according to the symptoms they produce.

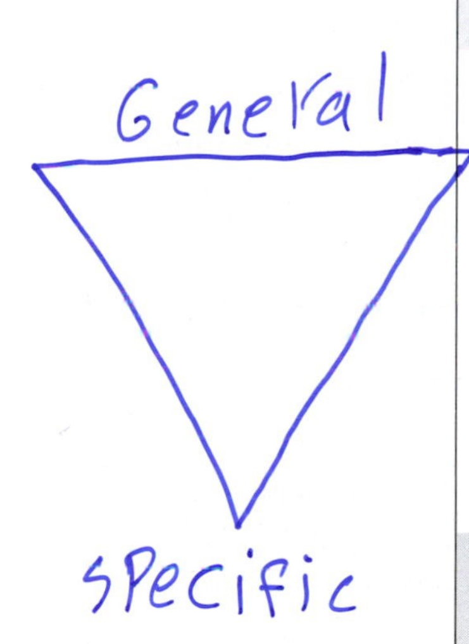

2. **Employing the funnel method.** (practiced in Unit 3) This is probably the most common technique to attract the reader. An introduction that uses the funnel method begins with general ideas about the topic. These ideas gradually become more and more focused until they reach their most specific and focused point in the thesis statement. The funnel method is very common in academic writing. It is not always the most attention-getting method, but it is very effective in introducing readers to complex topics.

Example:

Life in the twenty-first century is full of new challenges and opportunities. The pace of change in all areas of daily life makes it difficult to put these challenges and opportunities into perspective. Nevertheless, as the new millennium begins, it is important to take stock of where we have been, where we are today, and where we are going. One of the most obvious places to begin this process is by reviewing the evolution and impact of technology—the technology of the past, technology today, and, perhaps most important of all, the likely technology of our future.

3. **Using a relevant quotation.** (practiced in Unit 4) Writers who use this technique are careful to choose quotations written by authorities or by someone who says something especially relevant to their topic. They can then follow this quotation with related background information, which leads into the thesis statement.

Example:

"Life is just a bowl of cherries." This well-known, **anonymous** quotation is the **motto** of the optimist, the well-adjusted. It implies that life is full of "tasty" good things, ripe for the choosing, if only you **avail** yourself of the opportunity to pick from among them. However, what if you can't? What if life's cherries are there for the picking, but they always seem out of your reach. What if, for reasons you cannot comprehend, you cannot bring yourself to take advantage of the good things in life, only seeing life as a series of ever-worsening bad happenings. Such is the world of the clinically depressed. Depression strikes an increasing number of people each year, and its effects can be **devastating.**

anonymous: unknown

motto: special saying

avail (oneself) of: make use of

devastating: very harmful

4. **Making a startling or dramatic observation or describing a scene in a dramatic, humorous, or otherwise interesting way.** (practiced in Unit 5) Further background information then follows the "dramatic" hook of this opening, which then leads to the thesis statement.

Example:

He pounds down the court, ball in hands. **Deftly** sidestepping every obstacle in his path, he **barrels** toward the net. Nothing can stop him now. He leaps. For a split second, time stops, and this incredible athlete appears to be suspended in mid-air, his feet at least five feet above the floor. Then, suddenly, time starts again and the crowd begins to roar. Michael Jordan has done it again. He has made an extremely difficult **feat** seem effortless and natural, as though he were born with the ability to leap tall buildings in a single bound. The true story of this athlete's rise to stardom, however, is one of long suffering, hard work, and seemingly endless obstacles.

deftly: with great skill

barrel: move forward with strength

feat: achievement; accomplishment

5. **Turning an argument "on its head."** (practiced in Unit 7) This fairly sophisticated attention-getting introduction begins with a sentence or two presenting a point of view that is really the opposite of what the writer wants to say. At the end of this introduction, the writer overturns this idea completely and presents the thesis statement, which is the opposite of what he or she started with. This type of introduction is especially useful when the purpose of the essay is to give an opinion or make an argument.

Example:

American children are exposed to and **take part in** competitive sports starting at a very early age. By participating in such sports as football, tennis, and basketball, **proponents** claim, children learn the skills necessary to survive in today's fiercely competitive world. You only have to scratch the surface, however, to see how damaging competitive sports really are to the **overall** psychological development of children.

take part in: participate in

proponent: someone in favor of something

overall: general

EXERCISE 9

The Introduction and the Thesis Statement

Read the introduction and answer the questions.

"You are what you eat." This saying is true, to a great degree, for all of us. Most of the food we take in acts as fuel and is gradually digested and converted to the muscle and other types of tissue in our bodies. However, recent research has confirmed that some foods do more than merely contribute to our physical health; some foods are important to our emotional health as well. These foods are referred to by doctors and psychologists as "mood foods" or "comfort foods," and their importance to our overall health cannot be overestimated. The process by which mood foods act on our bodies to relieve stress and to promote an overall feeling of well-being is a three-step process.

1. Which "hook" technique is used in this introduction?

 ____

2. What is the thesis statement? Write it here.

 ____

 ____

3. Is this a direct or an indirect thesis statement?

 ____

The Body of the Essay

The **body** of an essay contains enough paragraphs to explain, discuss, or prove the essay's thesis statement. In each body paragraph the writer should discuss one aspect of the essay's main topic. Each body paragraph has its own topic sentence, supporting sentences, and a transition or concluding sentence. To ensure unity and coherence, good writers arrange the body paragraphs in logical order and join them with appropriate transition expressions that make them read smoothly.

EXERCISE 10

Topic Sentences for Body Paragraphs

Read each thesis statement. Then write two possible topic sentences for body paragraphs based on the thesis statement.

1. Four major components make up the marketing mix of any successful business: the product itself, the product price, the means of product distribution, and the means of product promotion.

 Topic Sentence for Body Paragraph 1: ______________________________

 ____

 Topic Sentence for Body Paragraph 2: ______________________________

 ____

2. Depression strikes an increasing number of people each year, and its effects can be devastating.

   Topic Sentence for Body Paragraph 1: ______________________________

   ____

   Topic Sentence for Body Paragraph 2: ______________________________

   ____

3. You only have to scratch the surface to see how damaging competitive sports really are to the overall psychological development of children.

   Topic Sentence for Body Paragraph 1: ______________________________

   ____

   Topic Sentence for Body Paragraph 2: ______________________________

   ____

Essay Conclusions

The conclusion in an essay is the last paragraph or two. One purpose of all conclusions is to signal the end of the essay. Here are some other purposes for conclusions:

IMPORTANT NOTE:

One thing you should NOT do in a conclusion is introduce and begin discussing a new topic. If you do, you will leave the reader with an unfinished feeling and distract from the unity of the essay.

- to add coherence by summarizing or restating the essay subtopics
- to add coherence by restating the essay thesis
- to leave the reader with the writer's final opinion
- to make a prediction or suggestion about the topic of the essay

EXERCISE 11

Conclusions: Purposes

Read the introduction and the conclusions. Then answer the questions.

Introduction: American children are exposed to and take part in competitive sports starting at a very early age. By participating in such sports as football, tennis, and basketball, proponents claim, children learn the skills necessary to survive in today's fiercely competitive world. You only have to scratch the surface, however, to see how damaging competitive sports really are to the overall psychological development of children.

Conclusion I: As has been demonstrated above, competitive sports can cause severe psychological damage to children. Research shows that, in a society that overvalues the "competitive edge," children can easily lose self-confidence and self-motivation when they are forced to engage in competitive sports at which they cannot succeed. In addition, children who are particularly successful in the competitive arena can develop aggressive tendencies which can manifest themselves in adult life as hostility and lack of empathy.

1. What purposes does this conclusion have? (Circle all that apply.)
   a To add coherence by restating the essay's thesis statement.
   b. To add coherence by restating important essay subtopics.
   c. To leave the reader with the writer's opinion.

Conclusion II: As has been demonstrated above, competitive sports can cause severe psychological damage to children. In a society which overvalues the "competitive edge," children can easily lose self-confidence and self-motivation when they are forced to engage in competitive sports at which they cannot succeed. In addition, children who are particularly successful in the competitive arena can develop aggressive tendencies which can manifest themselves in adult life as hostility and lack of empathy. In my view, this concentration on competition has become an epidemic in American culture. If something is not done in the near future to curb the American appetite for competitive sports, the youth of today will be unable to function as caring, productive members of the adult world of tomorrow.

2. What new purpose(s) have now been added to this conclusion? (Circle all that apply.)
   a. To restate the essay's thesis statement.
   b. To make a prediction about the essay's topic.
   c. To leave the reader with the writer's opinion.

3. Which of these two conclusions do you find the most interesting and effective? Why?

____

____

____

____

EXERCISE 12

Unity in Conclusions

Read each thesis statement, the topic sentences for the body paragraphs of the essay, and the conclusion. Some conclusions have unity. Others include sentences that introduce new topics and do not have unity. Cross out any sentences in the conclusion that do not belong. (If you want further practice with paragraph writing, develop the topic sentence for each body paragraph into a full paragraph.)

1. *Thesis Statement:* Many facts about the personal life of Albert Einstein surprise us when we first learn about them.

   Topic sentences for body paragraphs:

   a. His treatment of women is surprising.
   b. His social awkwardness is surprising.
   c. Some of his political views are surprising.

Conclusion: People are often quite surprised to hear these aspects of Einstein's personal life. When they learn of them, they sometimes ask themselves such questions as: How could such a great scientist have such disregard for the women in his life? What caused this super-intellect to be so awkward in the most basic of social situations? And, how could this man whose science led almost directly to the development of the atom bomb be so opposed to war? Einstein, who loved all things simple, would be pleased with the simplicity of the answers to these questions: for all his greatness, Albert Einstein was still a human being subject to all of the same strengths and weaknesses as the rest of humankind. Nobody is perfect. Many other scientists, including Robert Oppenheimer, also had imperfect personal lives.

2. *Thesis statement:* According to health and fitness experts, snowshoeing has recently become a favorite winter sport among college students for three reasons: it is inexpensive, it is not dangerous, and it is a quiet, calming activity.

   Topic sentences for body paragraphs:

   a. Snowshoeing costs very little, making it affordable even for students with no income.
   b. Compared to skiing and snowboarding, snowshoeing is quite safe.
   c. Finally, many students like snowshoeing because it is a quiet sport that allows them to appreciate the calm and peacefulness of winter outdoors.

Conclusion: For all of the reasons discussed above, snowshoeing is becoming more and more popular among college-age students as a winter sport. Health and fitness experts recommend it to anyone who is looking for an affordable, safe, and quiet way to work off energy and enjoy the great outdoors during the long winter months.

3. *Thesis statement:* There are five important, albeit time-consuming, steps to successfully painting a room.

   Topic sentences for body paragraphs:

   a. First, all exposed surfaces that you don't want to paint need to be protected.
   b. Next, you need to prepare the surfaces that you do want to paint.
   c. "Cutting in" with a small brush is the first step in the actual painting.
   d. Once you have cut in, you can use a roller to paint the large surfaces.
   e. Cleaning up is the final step, and it is also very important.

Conclusion: As you can see, it is important to work carefully and methodically when you are painting a room. If you patiently follow the five steps outlined, you will have a beautiful product to show for your labor, and you can sit back, relax, and enjoy your beautiful room for years to come. The initial investment of a little extra time makes it all worthwhile in the end.

PART B

The Writing Process: Practice Writing an Essay

Objectives	In Part B, you will:
Prewriting:	brainstorm ideas about a topic
Planning:	use an outline to organize your introduction, body, and conclusion
Partner Feedback:	review classmates' outlines and analyze feedback
First Draft:	write an introduction, a body, and a conclusion
Partner Feedback:	review classmates' essays and analyze feedback
Final Draft:	use feedback to write a final draft of your essay

The Writing Process: Writing Assignment

Your assignment is to write an original essay of four to five paragraphs describing a person you admire. The person can be someone you know well or someone you don't know at all. Follow the steps in the writing process in this section.

Mother Teresa

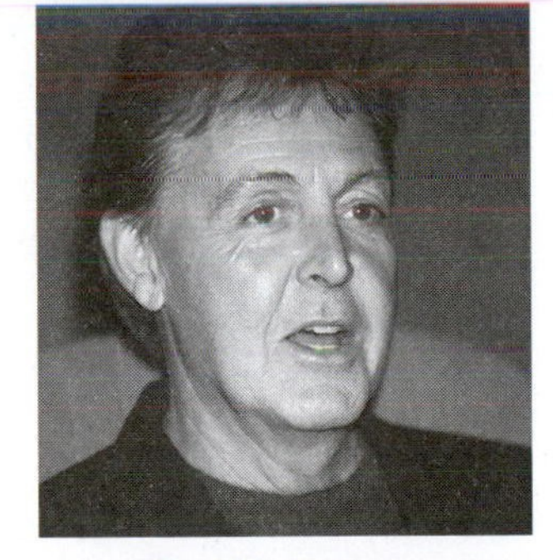
Paul McCartney

Grandmother

Mr. Kelley

Prewriting: Brainstorming

Brainstorming can help you get ideas for writing. You can brainstorm with a group or a partner—which can often generate more ideas faster—or you can brainstorm by yourself. To brainstorm, think of as many ideas as possible about a topic. Write the ideas as they come to you without evaluating, connecting, or editing them.

For this essay assignment, choose a person you admire. On a separate sheet of paper, quickly write whatever comes to mind about this person: What does he or she look like? Why do you admire this person? What do you know about this person? Don't worry about ranking or sequencing your ideas for now. Just try to think of as many ideas as you can.

Planning: Outlining

The next step is to organize and plan your essay. You will also generate more ideas in this step. One of the most effective ways to organize ideas is to prioritize them and make an outline.

Prioritizing and Connecting Ideas from Your Brainstorming

Read over your brainstorming ideas. Which ideas go together? Which ones are the most important? Divide your ideas into three or four major groups and use them to fill in the outline that follows. Eliminate ideas that don't seem important or useful.

EXERCISE 13

OUTLINING

Before you fill in this outline, try to think of a thesis statement and a hook for your essay. If you can't think of these right now, don't worry. You can come back to them later.

ESSAY OUTLINE

Topic: ____________________

I. Introductory Paragraph Using One of the Techniques in Part A (pp. 15–17)
   A. Hook and Background Information

   ____

   B. Thesis Statement

   ____

II. Body Paragraph 1
   A. Topic Sentence

   ____

   B. Supporting Details

   ____

III. Body Paragraph 2
 A. Topic Sentence

 ____

 B. Supporting Details

 ____

IV. Body Paragraph 3 (optional)
 A. Topic Sentence

 ____

 B. Supporting Details

 ____

V. Concluding Paragraph with Clear Purpose(s) and Link to Thesis

 A. ______________________________

 ____

 B. ______________________________

 ____

Partner Feedback Form 1

Exchange outlines with another student. Read your partner's outline and answer the questions on Partner Feedback Form 1: Unit 1, p. 219, in Appendix 3. Discuss your partner's reactions to your outline. Make notes about anything you need to change before you write your paper. For more information about giving partner feedback, see Appendix 2, p. 218, Guidelines for Partner Feedback.

First Draft

You are now ready to write the first draft of your essay. Review your outline and any comments from your partner before you begin.

EXERCISE 14

Writing the Introduction

Write an introduction for your topic, using your outline and the feedback you received from your partner. Use one of the introductory techniques explained on pp. 15–17. End your introduction with a well-constructed thesis statement. When you finish, use this checklist to review your work.

Introduction Checklist

	YES	NO
▸ Did I use a hook?	❑	❑
▸ Does my introduction flow logically from general to more specific?	❑	❑
▸ Does my thesis statement provide the reader with a clear guide for the rest of the essay?	❑	❑
▸ Is the purpose of my essay clear?	❑	❑

What is it? ______________________________

EXERCISE 15

Writing Body Paragraphs

Review your outline and your introduction. Then write the body paragraphs. Remember that each paragraph should be about something mentioned in the thesis statement. When you finish, use this checklist to review your work.

Body Paragraph Checklist

	YES	NO
▸ Does each paragraph in my essay treat only one main idea?	❑	❑
▸ Does each contain a topic sentence with a clear controlling idea?	❑	❑
▸ Does each paragraph end with a logical concluding sentence?	❑	❑
▸ Do my body paragraphs all relate to and support the essay's thesis statement?	❑	❑
▸ Are all the supporting sentences in my body paragraphs relevant to the topic? That is, do they have unity?	❑	❑
▸ Are my body paragraphs arranged in a logical order? That is, do they have coherence?	❑	❑

EXERCISE 16

Writing a Conclusion

Review again your essay outline, introduction, and body. Then write a conclusion for your essay. When you finish, use this checklist to review your work.

Conclusion Checklist

	YES	NO
▸ Does my conclusion successfully signal the end of my essay?	❑	❑
▸ Does my conclusion add coherence to the essay by		
a. restating the essay thesis?	❑	❑
b. summarizing or restating the essay subtopics?	❑	❑
▸ Does my conclusion:		
a. leave the reader with my final opinion?	❑	❑
b make a prediction or suggestion about the essay's topic?	❑	❑

Partner Feedback Form 2

Exchange essays with another student. Read your partner's essay and answer the questions on Partner Feedback Form 2: Unit 1, p. 221, in Appendix 3. Discuss your partner's reactions to your essay. Make notes about anything you need to change before you write your second draft. For more information about giving partner feedback, see Appendix 2, p. 218, Guidelines for Partner Feedback.

Final Draft

Carefully revise your essay using all the feedback you have received: partner feedback review of your outline and essay, instructor comments, and any evaluation you have done yourself. Use the following checklist to do a final check of your essay. In addition, try reading your essay aloud. This can help you find awkward-sounding sentences and punctuation errors. When you have finished, add a title to your essay and neatly type your final draft. See Appendix 4, p. 246, for information about writing titles.

Final Draft Checklist

	YES	NO
▶ Does my introduction have an effective hook?	❑	❑
▶ Did I include a thesis statement that contains a clear topic and controlling idea?	❑	❑
▶ Does each of my body paragraphs have a clear topic sentence?	❑	❑
▶ Does each of my body paragraphs treat one subtopic?	❑	❑
▶ Did I use transition expressions between body paragraphs to help make the essay coherent?	❑	❑
▶ Does my concluding paragraph have clear purposes?	❑	❑
▶ Does my concluding paragraph successfully signal the end of my essay?	❑	❑
▶ Does my entire essay have unity and coherence?	❑	❑
▶ Does my essay have a title?	❑	❑

Additional Writing Assignments from the Academic Disciplines

Beginning with the Prewriting activity on p. 24, use the writing process to write another essay. Choose a topic from the following list.

SUBJECT	*WRITING TASK*
Business	Write about the company in your hometown that employs the most people. How did this company get so big? What is its history?
Science	Describe the duckbill platypus (or some other animal you are interested in). Write about its physical characteristics as well as its habitat and habits.
Technology	What is the impact of the Internet on third world countries? Give your opinion.
Literature	Choose a novel that you like. Explain the plot and why you like it so much.

UNIT 2

Blueprints for

CLASSIFICATION ESSAYS

PART A

Blueprints for Classification Essays

Objectives	**In Part A, you will:**
Analysis:	learn about organizing principles in classification essays
Unity and Coherence:	
Unity	learn to classify topics according to category
Coherence: Transition Expressions	learn to use *one/another/a third (fourth, etc.)* + classifying word
Grammar Focus:	study and practice passive voice
Sentence Check:	study and practice adjective clauses
Practice:	practice classifying information

What Is a Classification Essay?

Writers use **classification** essays to group items according to their similarities and differences. Classification involves more than just making a list of items. When you classify, you impose order on the list. To decide on the order to use, you choose a **principle of organization.** This is the guideline or method that divides items into groups. For example, the paragraph "Writing for a Purpose" in Exercise 1, Unit 1 (p. 3) classifies *paragraphs* and *essays.* The principle of organization is according to their *purpose.* This organizing principle allows the writer to divide paragraphs and essays into different groups or categories based on the purposes for which they are written.

Classification is common in professional and academic writing. For example, scientists classify types of genes; business people categorize marketing strategies; dancers classify dance steps. The same set of items can be classified in different ways using different principles of organization. Study this example:

Items to be classified: Cars

Possible principles of organization: size, price, power, comfort, speed, safety

EXERCISE

CLASSIFICATION: PRINCIPLES OF ORGANIZATION

Determine the principle of organization for each of the following items and their categories. Write the principle in the blank. The first one is done for you.

1. **boats:** fiberglass, wood, metal

   Boats can be classified according to

   what they are made of.

2. **cities:** more than 5 million people, between 1 million and 5 million people, between 500,000 and 1 million people, fewer than 500,000 people

   We can classify cities into four groups according to

   their PoPulotion.

3. **beds:** twin, double, queen, and king

   There are four major tbPes

   of beds.

4. **chocolate:** sweet, semi-sweet, bitter

   Chocolate can be classified into three types according to

   the amount of sweetness.

5. **chocolate:** white, milk brown, dark brown

   Chocolate can be classified into three types according to

   its color.

EXERCISE

CLASSIFICATION: PRINCIPLES OF ORGANIZATION AND CATEGORIES

For each group, think of two different principles of organization and list several categories for each. The first one is done for you.

1. **dogs**

   a. Principle of organization 1: size

   Categories: miniature, small, medium-sized, large

   b. Principle of organization 2: hunting breeds

   Categories: Retrievers, Spaniels, Labradors

2. **friends**

   a. Principle of organization 1: tbPes of friends

   ____

Categories: ______________________________

____

b. Principle of organization 2: ______________________________

____

Categories: ______________________________

____

3. **teachers**

a. Principle of organization 1: ______________________________

____

Categories: ______________________________

____

b. Principle of organization 2: ______________________________

____

Categories: ______________________________

____

Unity in Classification Essays

To maintain unity in classification essays, it is important to use only one organizing principle when you classify the items in a group. If you use more than one, the classification system breaks down, and your essay will lose unity. (See Unit 1, pp. 4–5 and 21–22, for more information about unity.) For example, you might classify flowers according to their color: red, orange, yellow, purple, blue, etc. If you then include a group labeled "tall," you will have changed the principles of classification and will confuse your reader.

EXERCISE 3

Principles of Organization and Unity

Determine the principle of organization for each list. Write it on the blank. Draw a line through the category that does not belong. The first one is done for you.

1. **houses:** brick, stone, wooden, concrete, ~~small~~

Principle of organization: according to what they are made of

2. **letters:** personal, business, long

   Principle of organization: ______________________________

3. **television programs:** sitcoms, dramas, interesting, soap operas, talk shows, mini-series, newscasts, sports shows

   Principle of organization: ______________________________

4. **sports:** contact, team, individual

   Principle of organization: ______________________________

5. **coffee:** Espresso, Brazilian, Colombian, Hawaiian, Kenyan

   Principle of organization: ______________________________

Coherence in Classification Essays

As discussed in Unit 1 (pp. 5–8), writers use many techniques for adding coherence to paragraphs and essays. Effective use of transition expressions is one of the most important of these techniques. This section explains how to use several transition expressions that are especially useful in classification essays.

Transition Expressions: *one/another/a third (fourth, etc.)* + classifying word

one **+ classifying word**

Function: begins the classification process; gives the first category

Use: *One* is a determiner and is followed by a classifying word such as *type* or *category* or by another classifying noun or pronoun which specifies the organizing principle.

Examples: There are several types of cars, depending on their size. **One type** is the compact car.

Flowers are often categorized according to their color. **One** popular **color** is red.

another **+ classifying word**

Function: to signal the introduction of a category that comes after another category.

Use: Like *one, another* is a determiner and is followed by a classifying word such as *type,* or *category* or by another classifying noun or pronoun that specifies the organizing principle.

Examples: **Another type** of car is the mid-sized car.

Another very popular **color** for flowers is blue.

(continued)

(continued)

a third (fourth, etc.) + **classifying word**

Function: continues introducing categories in a classification system in a sequence

Use: *Third, fourth, fifth, etc.* are ordinal numbers. In classification writing, they come before nouns to help impose order on the categories.

Examples: **A third type** of car is the luxury-sized car.

A fourth flower **color** often found in gardens is yellow.

Blueprint Classification Essays

In this section, you will read and analyze two sample classification essays. These essays can act as blueprints when you write your own classification essay in Part B.

Blueprint Classification Essay 1: Amazing Animals

PREREADING DISCUSSION QUESTIONS

1. *What is the most unusual animal you have ever seen? Why was it so unusual?*
2. *Which animals do you think are the best at protecting themselves? At hunting? At being good parents?*

EXERCISE 4

Reading and Answering Questions

Read the classification essay. Fill in the blanks with transition expressions from the list. Then answer the post-reading discussion questions.

A third amazing animal category
Another category
One amazing animal survivor category

Amazing Animals

adept: skillful
assassins: killers

1 Who are the most **adept** escape artists on earth? The most effective **assassins**? The most devoted parents? You might expect these distinctions to go to members of our own noble species, homo sapiens, who have worked long and hard to perfect the art of survival. In fact, however, prizes in each of these categories might well go not to human beings at all, but to some amazing members of the animal kingdom. Three groups of amazing animal survivors are particularly impressive, and they can be classified according to the types of survival behaviors they exhibit.

(continued)

(continued)

2 ______________________________ is the escape artist. In order to survive, members of the animal kingdom must become experts at escaping their **predators,** and they have developed some extraordinary techniques for doing so. One prime example of an animal escape artist is the horned lizard, which can actually squirt blood from its eyeballs to frighten predators away. The foul-tasting blood causes predators like foxes and coyotes to drop their prey, allowing the lizard to make a hasty escape. The sea cucumber, which lives in the ocean, is another amazing escape artist. It will actually **eject** its entire digestive system as a **decoy** and then scurry away unharmed from its predators. This would be a drastic measure for a human, but for a sea cucumber, it's all part of a day's work at survival. Once safely away from its **foe,** the cucumber simply **regenerates** its internal digestive organs.

horned lizard

predators: hunters

eject: throw out

decoy: something used to fool predators

foe: enemy

regenerates: grows back again

prey: victims; those who are hunted by predators

abound: are numerous

rival: compete with

3 ______________________________ of amazing animal is the expert predator. Predation is an important part of animal survival, and some animals have developed particular talents for it. The tiny black and silver archer fish, for example, can spit water up to a distance of five feet to catch its prey—bugs resting on riverbanks and in overhanging plants. The water knocks the bugs into the water, where they are gobbled up by this sharpshooter, who rarely misses its target. The carnivorous sponge, which lives in dark Mediterranean caves, has developed tentacles covered with microscopic, Velcro-like hooks. These hooks snag crustaceans that swim by. Within 24 hours, the sponge's tentacles envelop the **prey,** trapping it and burying it alive.

archer fish

4 ______________________________ is the devoted parent, and examples of this category **abound** in nature. One particularly devoted dad is the chivalrous emperor penguin. This father braves the frigid Antarctic winter without a bite to eat for two months to incubate his mate's single egg. During this time, papa penguin loses up to 50 percent of his body weight, all for the sake of protecting his unborn chick. The Surinam toad mom is another devoted parent. She carries her babies around on her back from the time they are eggs until they are well beyond the tadpole stage—for up to 80 days. She might play "taxicab" to up to 25 babies at one time, but she never complains!

Emperor Penguin

5 Members of the animal kingdom clearly demonstrate extraordinary survival behaviors. Be they mammal, amphibian, reptile, bird, or bug, they certainly **rival** humans in the amazing creativity and effectiveness they exhibit at the art of staying alive.

Adapted from: www.discovery.com/stories/nature/supernature/supernature.html [January 20, 2001]. Used by permission of Discovery Communications, Inc.

POSTREADING DISCUSSION QUESTIONS

1. *What is the thesis statement of this essay? Write it here.*

   ____

2. *What kind of hook or essay introduction technique does the writer use in the introduction? (See Unit 1, pp. 15–17 for a list of introductory techniques.)*

   ____

3. *What is the writer classifying?*

   ____

4. *What is the principle of organization?*

   ____

5. *Write down each category discussed in the essay.*

   Category 1 ______________________________________

   Category 2 ______________________________________

   Category 3 ______________________________________

   Does each category follow the same principle of organization? That is, does this classification essay have unity?

   ____

6. *This essay uses examples to give details about each category. List these examples.*

   Examples for Category 1

   ____

   ____

   ____

   Examples for Category 2

   ____

   ____

   ____

   Examples for Category 3

   ____

   ____

   ____

7. *Underline the controlling idea of each body paragraph in the essay. Does each body paragraph address only one of the subtopics?*

____

8. *Does the conclusion successfully signal the end of the essay?*

____

9. *What are the other purposes of the conclusion? Does it achieve these purposes?*

____

____

Blueprint Classification Essay 2: Ten Thousand Teas

PREREADING DISCUSSION QUESTIONS

1. *What is your favorite beverage? Why?*
2. *In what ways are black tea, green tea, and oolong tea the same? Different?*
3. *Which do you prefer—black tea, green tea, or oolong tea? Why?*

EXERCISE 5

Reading and Answering Questions

Read the classification essay and answer the questions.

Ten Thousand Teas

1 An eighth century Chinese literary man poetically numbered the different types of tea at "ten thousand and a thousand." The Chinese for 10,000—萬—is the **vernacular** for something more than mere numbers, however. It **conveys** greatness and superiority. "Ten thousand and a thousand" expresses "super-excellence," and tea, an evergreen

(continued)

vernacular: everyday language

conveys: communicates

(continued)

plant in the Camellia family (Camellia Sinensis), is considered by much of the world's population to be the most excellent beverage available.

How many types of tea are there, really, and what determines these types? Are there really "ten thousand and a thousand" different teas, as the Chinese poet claimed? Is the Earl Gray you drank this morning different from the English Breakfast you drank this afternoon?

In fact, there are only three major types of tea—black, green, and oolong—and the difference among them lies not in their origins but in the methods by which they are processed.

2 Making black tea is an involved process and takes great skill. First the leaves are withered in the sun. Then they are usually rolled, often by hand. The rolling breaks down the **membranes** of the leaves to activate a natural chemical reaction. The leaves are next **fermented** by letting them dry on woven trays, or by laying them out in a cool place. Oxygen works on the leaves, helping to release their essential oils. This drying takes several hours, during which the leaves become reddened and let off a nutty **aroma.** Once the leaves have fermented for a sufficient length of time, the tea is fired in large woks or in an oven; this process causes the fermentation to cease. At this point, the leaves, which are about 80 percent dry, are then completely dried with more firing of wood or charcoal. Black teas are rich and full-bodied. Perfecting tea that gives just the right amount of light pungency and full flavor while allowing for **multiple infusions** is an art form.

membranes: outside surfaces

fermented: chemically changed; broken down

aroma: smell; odor

multiple infusions: more than one use of same amount of tea

3 Green teas are not dried before processing, nor are they fermented. The fresh tea leaves that are used for green tea are quickly steamed to halt bacterial and enzyme action common in fermentation. Next, the leaves are machine rolled lightly to give them a curl, to break up leaf cells, and to free juices and enzymes. Finally, green tea leaves are fired or heat dried. Throughout this process, leaf color is preserved as yellowish-green or green. Because the green tea leaf is not fermented, its chemical makeup is not altered as in black tea processing. This preserves the medicinal and natural flavors so cherished in green teas.

4 Oolong teas fall in between green and black teas in the degree of fermentation. Tea leaves used for oolong are wilted in the sun just as those for black teas are. They are then tossed by spinning in cylindrical bamboo woven baskets. This "bruises" the leaves, which helps promote a brief fermenting process. These two processes are repeated until the leaves become almost **transparent** and start to yellow or redden along the edges, which is a sign of the beginnings of fermentation. The center, however, remains green and the degree of fermentation is far less than

transparent: clear; colorless

(continued)

(continued)

that of black tea. As a final step, oolong tea processors roll the large leaves into nugget shapes that **unfurl** when they are **steeped.** Oolong teas are known for their flowery aromas that soothe and heal.

unfurl: open up

steeped: soaked in water

5 Since ancient times, tea has been a preferred beverage for much of the world's population. As its popularity has grown, its basic makeup has been enhanced to suit the "ten thousand and a thousand" different human tastes. The three basic types of tea have been blended, scented, and packaged in many different ways. They can now be found flavored with flowers and herbs or **adorned** with berries and grains. They are sometimes perfumed with oils and sometimes even **speckled** with tiny flakes of precious metals. It is somehow reassuring to know that each of these "ten thousand and a thousand" types of tea nevertheless comes from one of only three possible humble beginnings, each of which can be trusted for its soothing and healing properties.

adorned: decorated

speckled: mixed; dotted

Adapted from: www.taooftea.com/cgi-bin/teashop.cgi? January 2001 and C. Schafer, V. Schafer, *Teacraft* (San Francisco: Yerba Buena Press, 1975).

POSTREADING DISCUSSION QUESTIONS

1. *What is the thesis statement of this essay? Write it here.*

   ____

2. *How many subtopics are there?* ______________ *What are they?*

   ____

3. *Where does the writer use questions?*

   ____

   Do you think they are effective in this position in the essay? Why or why not? ____

   ____

4. *Underline the controlling idea of each body paragraph in the essay. Does each body paragraph address one of the subtopics?*

   ____

5. *Does the conclusion successfully signal the end of the essay?*

   ____

6. *What are the other purposes of the conclusion? Does it achieve these purposes?* ______________________________

____

7. *Does the entire essay have unity and coherence? If not, what should be done to add unity and coherence?*

____

8. *What is classified in this essay? What principle of organization does the writer use?*

____

9. *What is primarily used in this essay to give details about the categories? (Circle one.)*

   a. examples *b. descriptions of a process*

   c. details of a story *d. the author's opinion*

Grammar Focus and Sentence Check

In this part of the unit, the first grammar instruction, Grammar Focus, highlights English grammar points that are common problems for ESL students. The second grammar instruction, Sentence Check, will help you write better sentences of different types to include in your essays.

Grammar Focus: Passive Voice

Sentences in the **passive voice** have the same basic meaning as sentences in the active voice. However, passive and active sentences present information in different ways. In active voice sentences, the subject is the performer or **agent** of the action.

Example: **I** ordered the tickets.

In passive voice sentences, the subject is the **receiver** of the action.

Receiver

Example: **The tickets** were ordered.

The topic of a sentence—the person or thing the sentence is about—is generally in the subject position. The passive voice allows us to treat the receiver of the action as the topic and put it in the subject position.

The passive voice is used more in writing than in speech. It is common in news reports where it helps create an objective or impartial impression by distancing the reporter from the topic.

Example:

Little **is known** about the whereabouts of the terrorist. (news report)

The passive is also used in scientific and other academic writing, where agents are often less important than processes and results.

Example:

The experimental drug **was tested** for several years before it **was approved** by the medical community. (scientific writing)

The *By*-Phrase in Passive Sentences

If you include the subject, or agent, of an active sentence in the corresponding passive sentence, this subject occurs in a prepositional phrase beginning with *by*.

Examples:

Active voice: **The cats** destroyed the plants.

Passive voice: The plants were destroyed **by the cats.**

In the following cases, you should omit the *by*-phrase.

1. If the agent is unknown, unimportant, or unnecessary because of the context.

   Example: This cat **is trained** already. (We don't know or need to know who trained it.)

2. If the agent is a general subject (people, impersonal *you* or *they, someone, everyone*)

   Example: Wars **have been fought** since the dawn of humanity. (by people)

3. If you do not want to mention, or even indicate, an agent.

   Example: A mistake **was made,** but let's forget it. (The writer does not want to place blame on someone, even though he or she may know who made the mistake.)

Forming the Passive Voice

To form the passive voice, use a form of *be* + the past participle of the main verb. The tense of the active sentence is used in the passive as well. Like active sentences, passive sentences can occur in any tense. Here are some examples.

Tense	Active Voice	Passive Voice
Simple Present	Someone eats the bread (every day.)	The bread is eaten (every day.)
Simple Past	Someone ate the bread.	The bread was eaten.
Future	Someone will/is going to eat the bread.	The bread will/is going to be eaten.
Present Progressive	Someone is eating the bread.	The bread is being eaten.
Past Perfect	Someone had eaten the bread.	The bread had been eaten.

EXERCISE

PASSIVE VOICE IN *TEN THOUSAND TEAS*

Reread "Ten Thousand Teas" on pp. 37–39. Underline all the passive verbs that you can find in the essay. Then answer these questions.

1. How many passive voice verbs did you find? ____________

   List them here. ______________________________

   ____

   ____

   ____

   ____

   ____

2. Do most of the passive voice sentences in this passage contain *by*-phrases? ______________________________

   Why or why not? ______________________________

   ____

   ____

   ____

   ____

EXERCISE

KEEPING THE TOPIC IN THE SUBJECT POSITION

*Sometimes the passive voice is needed to keep the topic in the subject position. Sometimes the active voice is needed. In each item below, decide which statement—**a** or **b**—better follows the sentence above it by keeping the topic in the subject position. Circle your choice. The first one is done for you.*

1. How would it feel to have the same name as a celebrity? Just ask Indiana University Professor Jack Nicholson.
   (a.) He has often been mistaken for the famous Hollywood actor who has the same name.
   b. People have mistaken him for the famous Hollywood actor who has the same name.
2. Once, when he went to pick up a pizza that he had ordered over the telephone,
   a. he was met by fans who wanted his autograph.
   b. fans who wanted his autograph met him.
3. They were surprised when they saw him,
   a. but he was asked by them to sign autographs anyway.
   b. but they asked him to sign autographs anyway.
4. He signed "Best wishes, Jack Nicholson" on several slips of paper.
   a. Then his pizza was taken home.
   b. Then he took his pizza home.
5. Another time, he made reservations at an exclusive resort. When he arrived there,
   a. he was told that he didn't have a reservation.
   b. someone told him that he didn't have a reservation.
6. The woman at the reservations desk had thought that Dr. Nicholson was joking about his name.
   a. For that reason, the reservation had been canceled by her.
   b. For that reason, she had canceled the reservation.
7. Despite all the problems it causes, Dr. Nicholson seems to have a good sense of humor about his name.
   a. He hasn't been stopped by it from enjoying life.
   b. It hasn't stopped him from enjoying life.

Sentence Check: Adjective Clauses

An **adjective clause** (also called a relative clause) modifies a noun. An adjective clause identifies, describes, or gives more information about the noun it modifies. Always put an adjective clause right after the noun it modifies.

Adjective clauses are *dependent clauses.* This means they cannot stand alone as sentences, and they must be connected to *independent clauses.* You can create a sentence with an adjective clause from two sentences if each sentence contains a noun that refers to the same person or thing. In the combined sentence, a relative pronoun replaces the second noun.

Example:

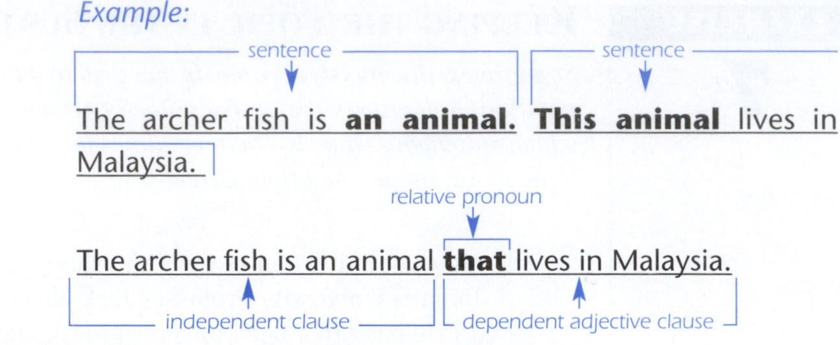

Relative Pronouns in Adjective Clauses

Adjective clauses begin with relative pronouns. The most common relative pronouns are *who, whom, whose, which,* and *that.* Some relative pronouns can be the subjects of adjective clauses. The subject relative pronouns are *who, which,* and *that.*

Example:

A person **who** makes good tea is a true artist!

Some relative pronouns can be the objects of relative clauses. The object relative pronouns are *who, whom, which,* and *that.* You can often omit the object relative pronoun (Ø = no relative pronoun).

Examples:

Object of *admire*

A scientist **whom/who/that/Ø** I admire studies Surinam toads.

Object of *love*

A toad **that/which/Ø** I love dearly is the Surinam toad.

The relative pronoun *whose* is a possessive like *my, her*, and *his.* You must always put a noun after *whose.*

Example:

Subject

I met the scientist **whose work** with toads has made him famous.

IMPORTANT NOTE:

- When you write an adjective clause, be careful not to include an extra pronoun.

Incorrect: The scientist *that* I like him studies Surinam toads.

Correct: The scientist *that* I like studies Surinam toads.

- Never omit a subject relative pronoun. Only an objective relative pronouns can be omitted.

Incorrect: A person makes great tea is my mother

Correct: A person *who* makes great tea is my mother.

EXERCISE

Practice with Relative Pronouns

Fill in the blanks with all the relative pronoun choices (who, whose, whom, which, that, (Ø)) *that are possible. The first one is done for you.*

1. The Amish are a group of religious people who/that live in the United States.
2. The life ____________ these people lead is one of simplicity and humility.
3. The Amish ____________ settlement is the largest are the Pennsylvania Amish.
4. The Amish ____________ have their settlement in Pennsylvania do not drive cars.
5. Instead, they have buggies ____________ are pulled by horses.

EXERCISE

Sentence Combining to Form Relative Clauses

Read each pair of sentences. Use the second sentence to form an adjective clause modifying the appropriate noun in the first sentence. Place the adjective clause where it makes sense in the sentence. More than one answer may be possible. The first one is done for you.

1. Last week I visited a zoo. The zoo was full of interesting animals.

   Last week I visited a zoo that was full of interesting animals. OR Last week I visited a zoo which was full of interesting animals.

desert lynx

2. One animal was a desert lynx. I saw the animal.

____

____

____

3. The desert lynx is a type of cat. This cat lives in North Africa.

____

____

____

4. Birds are in trouble if there is a desert lynx nearby. These birds fly near the ground.

____

____

____

5. Birds are captured quickly by this animal acrobat. Their wings dip too low.

____

____

____

Restrictive and Nonrestrictive Adjective Clauses

A **restrictive adjective clause** identifies the noun it modifies. It gives information that the reader needs in order to know who or what the noun refers to.

Example:

Scientists who study sea cucumbers are rare. (Certain kinds of scientists are rare, not all scientists.)

If you omit a restrictive adjective clause, you change the basic meaning of the sentence.

Example:

restrictive adjective clause

Scientists **who study sea cucumbers** are rare.

This sentence does not mean the same thing as:

Scientists are rare.

IMPORTANT NOTE:

- Because nonrestrictive adjective clauses are not necessary to the sense of the sentence, you always put commas around them.
- Never put commas around restrictive adjective clauses because they are necessary to the sense of the sentence.
- Use *that* only in restrictive adjective clauses. Do not use *that* in nonrestrictive clauses.

Correct: The kangaroo, which is an interesting animal, lives in Australia.

Incorrect: The kangaroo, that is an interesting animal, lives in Australia.

A **nonrestrictive adjective clause** adds information about the noun it modifies but is not needed for the sentence to make sense.

Example:

nonrestrictive adjective clause

Scientists, **who help us understand the world around us,** are important members of society.

If you omit a nonrestrictive adjective clause, you do not change the basic meaning of the sentence.

Example:

Scientists are important members of society. = Scientists are important members of society.

EXERCISE 10

Restrictive and Nonrestrictive Adjective Clauses

Read these sentences taken from the Blueprint essay Amazing Animals *in this unit. Each sentence contains an adjective clause. Underline each adjective clause and identify it as restrictive or nonrestrictive. Where it is possible to do so without losing the basic meaning, rewrite the sentence, omitting the adjective clause. The first one is done for you.*

1. One prime example of an animal escape artist is the horned lizard, which can actually squirt blood from its eyeballs to frighten predators away. nonrestrictive

   Rewrite?

   One prime example of an animal escape artist is the horned lizard.

2. The sea cucumber, which lives in the ocean, is another amazing escape artist. ____

   Rewrite?

   ____

   ____

3. The carnivorous sponge, which lives in dark Mediterranean caves, has developed tentacles covered with microscopic, Velcro-like hooks. ______________________

   Rewrite?

   ____

   ____

   ____

4. These hooks snag crustaceans that swim by.

   ____

   Rewrite?

   ____

   ____

   ____

EXERCISE 11

ADJECTIVE CLAUSE PUNCTUATION

Read these sentences with adjective clauses and add commas where they are needed.

1. Emily Dickinson who was a famous poet was very eccentric.
2. The woman that I saw last night at the opera looked just like my Aunt Rose.
3. Jack Kenney whom I don't know very well has been hired by our company.
4. One scientist whose work led to the development of the atomic bomb was J. Robert Oppenheimer.
5. They really enjoy music by Emmy Lou Harris who is a country-western musician.
6. On one side of the moon there is a crater that fascinates geologists.

EXERCISE 12

Editing Practice: Grammar Focus and Sentence Check Application

Read this passage carefully. Find and correct the eight passive voice and adjective clause errors. The first one is done for you.

Bowling is a sport that ~~it~~ is growing in popularity. It is enjoy by young and old, athletic and nonathletic, and competitive and noncompetitive people alike.

Although it might look easy, bowling is a sport who takes a certain amount of skill. The professional bowlers that you see in bowling competitions on television work hard to perfect their game. Their bowling skills must be practiced by them every day.

Bowling is sometimes described by bowlers as a very exciting and strenuous sport. However, most bowlers are interested in this sport more for the relaxation it provides than for the excitement. A person likes bowling a lot is my cousin George. He's just an average kind of guy and an average bowler. Average bowlers, that seem to love low-key fun and entertainment, are a growing group in the United States. Do you think that bowling which is becoming more and more popular could ever become more popular than baseball?

PART B

The Writing Process: Practice Writing a Classification Essay

Objectives	In Part B, you will:
Prewriting:	practice using a checklist to get ideas for writing
Planning:	use a tree diagram to organize and sequence ideas for classification
Partner Feedback:	review classmates' tree diagrams and analyze feedback
First Draft:	write a classification essay
	use posing questions as an introductory technique
Partner Feedback:	review classmates' essays and analyze feedback
Final Draft:	use feedback to write a final draft of your classification essay

The Writing Process: Writing Assignment

Before you look for a new job, it is important to think about the different types of jobs that might interest you. Your assignment is to write a classification essay about the types of jobs you would most enjoy. Give details about each type. Follow the steps in the writing process in this section.

The Helping Professions

Hands-On Jobs

Problem-Solving Jobs

Orderly, Mechanical Work

Creative and Artistic Jobs

Persuasive or Leadership Positions

Prewriting: Using a Checklist to Get Ideas

Completing a checklist about your topic can help you get started writing. Complete the checklist below.

Check ✔ each of the jobs that attracts you in some way. Check at least 15 jobs.

Job Inventory		
❑ Poet	❑ Farmer	❑ Marketing Person
❑ Cashier	❑ Nurse	❑ Counselor
❑ President	❑ Carpenter	❑ Photographer
❑ Word Processor	❑ Teacher	❑ Butler
❑ Lawyer	❑ Telephone Operator	❑ Social Worker
❑ Butcher	❑ Singer	❑ Historian
❑ Actor	❑ Police Officer	❑ Data Processor
❑ Homemaker	❑ Geneticist	❑ Architect
❑ Designer	❑ Coach	❑ Ticket Seller
❑ Researcher	❑ Doctor	❑ Plumber
❑ Veterinarian	❑ Social Worker	❑ Economist
❑ Pharmacist	❑ Bricklayer	❑ Gardener
❑ Dancer	❑ Movie Producer	❑ Flight Attendant
❑ Tax Examiner	❑ Politician	❑ Business Manager
❑ Mathematician	❑ Detective	❑ Race Car Driver
❑ Painter	❑ Dietician	❑ Airplane Pilot

Planning: Using a Tree Diagram

Now that you have chosen jobs that might interest you, organize them into categories. Use a tree diagram to do this. Hang the label for each type of job from the tree. Use labels from the pictures on page 50 for your categories, or create categories of your own. Hang details under each job category. Try to include similar details about each type of job. Your details might include such things as: personality traits needed for each job category, reasons why you like these types of jobs, values associated with these job types, and/or abilities needed for these jobs. Write a draft of your thesis statement at the bottom of your diagram. You can change it later if you need to.

Here is an example of how your tree diagram might look:

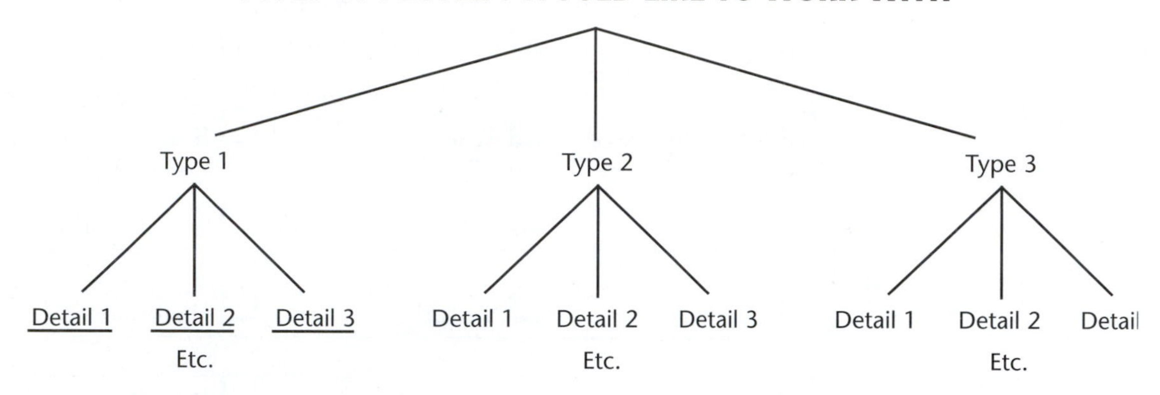

Draft of Thesis Statement: ____________________

Partner Feedback Form 1

Exchange tree diagrams with another student. Read your partner's diagram and answer the questions on Partner Feedback Form 1: Unit 2, p. 223 in Appendix 3. Discuss your partner's reactions to your tree diagram. Make notes about any parts you need to change before you write your paper. For more information about giving partner feedback, see Appendix 2, p. 218, Guidelines for Partner Feedback.

First Draft

You are now ready to write the first draft of your essay. Before you begin, review your tree diagram and any comments from your partner.

EXERCISE 13

WRITING THE INTRODUCTION

Write an introduction for your topic, using your tree diagram and the feedback you received from your partner. In the introduction to your essay, use the posing questions *technique as explained in Unit 1, p. 15. Both "Amazing Animals" on pp. 34–35 and "Ten Thousand Teas" on pp. 37–39 use this technique. You can use them as models if you want. End your introduction with a well-constructed thesis statement. When you finish, use the checklist to review your work.*

Introduction Checklist

	YES	NO
► Did I use an effective question or questions to hook my audience?	❑	❑
► Does my introduction flow logically from general to more specific?	❑	❑
► Does my thesis statement provide the reader with a clear guide for the rest of the essay?	❑	❑
► Is the purpose of my essay clear?	❑	❑

► What is it? ____________________

____

____

____

IMPORTANT NOTE:

Try to make your introductory question interesting—something that will take your reader by surprise or that you think he or she will want to know the answer to.

Examples: Who are the most adept escape artists on earth? The most effective assassins? The most devoted parents?

You can use more than one question in your hook, but keep your question or questions short. Long questions will lose your reader's attention.

Make sure you answer your question or questions as you write your essay!

EXERCISE 14

Writing Body Paragraphs

Look again at your tree diagram and your introduction. Then write the body paragraphs. Remember to discuss each category you mention in the thesis statement. When you finish, use the checklist to review your work.

Body Paragraph Checklist

	YES	NO
▸ Does each body paragraph in my essay treat only one main idea?	❑	❑
▸ Does each contain a topic sentence with a clear controlling idea?	❑	❑
▸ Do I use only one principle of classification in the body of my essay?	❑	❑
▸ Does each paragraph end with a logical concluding sentence?	❑	❑
▸ Do my body paragraphs all relate to and support the essay's thesis statement?	❑	❑
▸ Are all the supporting sentences in my body paragraphs relevant to the topic? That is, do they have unity?	❑	❑
▸ Are my body paragraphs arranged in a logical order? That is, do they have coherence?	❑	❑

EXERCISE 15

Writing a Conclusion

Review again your tree diagram, introduction, and body. Write a conclusion for your essay. When you finish, use the checklist to review your work.

Conclusion Checklist

	YES	NO
▸ Does my conclusion successfully signal the end of my essay?	❑	❑
▸ Does my conclusion add coherence to the essay by:	❑	❑
a. restating the essay thesis?	❑	❑
b. mentioning again the principle of organization and/or the items classified in my essay?	❑	❑
▸ Does my conclusion:		
a. leave the reader with my final thoughts?	❑	❑
b. make a prediction or suggestion about the essay's topic?	❑	❑

Partner Feedback Form 2

Exchange essays with another student. Read your partner's essay and answer the questions on Partner Feedback Form 2: Unit 2, p. 225–226, in Appendix 3. Discuss your partner's reactions to your essay. Make notes about any parts you need to change before you write your final draft. For more information about giving partner feedback, see Appendix 2, p. 218, Guidelines for Partner Feedback.

Final Draft

Carefully revise your essay using all the feedback you have received: partner feedback review of your outline and essay, instructor comments, and any evaluation you have done yourself. Use the following checklist to do a final check of your essay. In addition, try reading your essay aloud. This can help you find awkward-sounding sentences and punctuation errors. When you have finished, add a title to your essay, and neatly type your final draft. See Appendix 4, p. 246, for information about writing titles.

Final Draft Checklist

	YES	NO
▸ Will my introductory question(s) hook my audience?	❑	❑
▸ Did I include a thesis statement that contains a clear topic and controlling idea?	❑	❑
▸ What principle of organization did I use to classify people? Write it here. ______________________	❑	❑
▸ Did I use only one principle of organization?	❑	❑
▸ Did I use transition expressions, such as *one/another/a third* (*fourth, etc.*) + classifying word, between body paragraphs to help make the essay coherent?	❑	❑
▸ Did I use passive voice and adjective clauses correctly?	❑	❑
▸ Does each of my body paragraphs have a clear topic sentence?	❑	❑
▸ Does each of my body paragraphs treat one classification subtopic?	❑	❑
▸ Does my concluding paragraph have clear purposes?	❑	❑
▸ Does my concluding paragraph successfully signal the end of my essay?	❑	❑
▸ Does my entire essay have unity and coherence?	❑	❑
▸ Does my essay have a title?	❑	❑

Additional Writing Assignments from the Academic Disciplines

Beginning with the Prewriting activity on p. 51, use the writing process to write another classification essay. Choose a topic from the following list.

SUBJECT	*WRITING TASK*
Business	Classify job-hunting methods. What types of methods can you use to find a job? (for example, using the Web, talking to friends, looking in the newspaper, etc.)
Science	Choose a species of mammal and classify the subspecies within this species.
Technology	Classify the different types of disk operating systems commonly available to private consumers today.
Social science	Classify the types of adoption possible (domestic, international, from foster care, etc.)
Linguistics	Classify the languages of the world into the categories most commonly used by linguists.

UNIT 3

Blueprints for

PROCESS ESSAYS

PART A Blueprints for Process Essays

Objectives	**In Part A, you will:**
Analysis:	learn about instructional and analytical process essays
Unity and Coherence:	
Unity:	learn to include all the relevant steps/stages in process essays
Coherence:	
Chronological Order	learn about the importance of chronological order in process essays
Transition Expressions	learn to use *first* (*second, third,* etc.), *next, now, then,* and *finally; before, after, once, as soon as* and *while* + sentence; *during, over, between* + noun phrase.
Grammar Focus:	study and practice articles
Sentence Check:	study and practice adverb clauses
Practice:	practice explaining a process

What Is a Process Essay?

Writers use **process** essays to explain the steps or stages in processes or procedures. A process essay is organized **chronologically,** that is in order of time. Process essays describe steps or stages that follow each other in time. This time can be relatively short (the steps involved in winking your eye) or relatively long (the stages involved in the formation of river canyons).

Types of Process Essays

Process essays can be of two types: **instructional** and **analytical.** *Instructional process essays* are "how-to" essays. They instruct the reader about how to do something, for example, how to ride a bike, how to plan a vacation, or how to pass a difficult test. *Analytical process essays* tell the steps involved in how something works or how something happens or happened. Analytical process essays are often used in academic writing, for example, to explain the steps in an experiment. Anthropologists use this type of writing to explain, for example, the marriage customs of different cultures. Specialists in literature use analytical process essays to explain the steps they follow when analyzing poetry and prose. In instructional process essays, the reader is being taught how to recreate a process. In analytical process essays, the reader is learning about a process but is not necessarily expected to recreate that process.

EXERCISE 1

INSTRUCTIONAL AND ANALYTICAL PROCESSES

Identify each process essay thesis statement as instructional (I) or analytical (A). The first one is done for you.

I Follow this recipe and you'll end up with a heavenly angel food cake.

A The digestive process involves several related steps.

I All it takes to build a beautiful deck is the right tools and these easy-to-use guidelines.

I To test the chlorine in your swimming pool water, use this test kit and follow the instructions carefully.

A By 7:00 in the morning, a sheep rancher has already completed a series of very demanding chores to get his sheep ready for the day.

Introductions in Process Essays

As with other essay introductions, process essay introductions name the topic (the process to be described). They also give the reader information about the essay's organization (chronologically-ordered steps or stages). In process essays, the thesis statement is often very direct. It can be something as simple as "There are four steps in tying a shoe," or it can include a persuasive idea, as in "The four steps involved in tying a shoe can be quite difficult for a 5-year-old child." This statement would require the writer to both describe the process of shoe tying and discuss its difficulties for a young child.

One effective hook for process essays is the funnel method (see Unit 1, p. 15). You will review and practice this introductory technique in this unit.

Conclusions in Process Essays

The conclusion to a process essay, like all conclusions, should bring the essay to a close. It should have one or more of the purposes discussed in Unit 1, pp. 19–20. Often, the conclusion sums up the process and discusses its results.

Unity in Process Essays

It is sometimes a challenge to make your process essay unified—to decide what to include and what to omit. Your process should be complete and not leave out any important steps. However, make sure you don't have more information than you need, and be careful not to include irrelevant material. See Unit 1, pp. 4–5 and 21–22, for more about unity in essays.

EXERCISE 2

Missing Steps in a Process

In each list of steps below, one important step or stage is missing. Insert it where it belongs. The first one is done for you.

1. Planting a tree
    - Find a place for the tree.
    - Dig a hole the width and depth of the root ball.
    - Remove any covering from the root ball of the tree.
    - Put the tree in the hole.
    - Fill the hole back up again, and tamp the soil down around the tree.
2. Repairing a scratched compact disk (CD)
    - Listen to the CD and note where the worst skips are.
    -
    - Take out the CD, hold it by the edge, and wipe the shiny side gently with mild soap and water to remove dust and fingerprints. Rinse carefully.

- Using a lint-free cloth, dry the CD surface gently from the center to the outer edge. Do not use a circular motion.

- Now, hold the shiny side of the CD under a bright light and look for whitish scratches.

- Dampen the cloth and put some plain white toothpaste on the cloth.

- ____

- Listen to your CD and see if it is fixed. If not, start the process over.

Adapted from "How to Repair Scratched CDs", *Real Simple Magazine,* November 2001, p. 48

3. The water cycle

   - Warmth from the sun causes water to evaporate from surfaces of lakes, oceans, and rivers.

   - This water vapor rises and cools.

   - ____

   - The clouds become heavy with moisture.

   - The cycle begins again.

EXERCISE

Extra Information in a Process

Each list includes one or more irrelevant steps or stages. Draw a line through the irrelevant information. The first one is done for you.

1. Basic steps that scientists follow in using the Scientific Method of inquiry
   - They formulate a hypothesis and base a prediction on this hypothesis.
   - They test the hypothesis using one of a number of techniques.
   - ~~They usually enjoy their work.~~
   - They analyze the results of the tests.
   - They draw conclusions about the hypothesis.
   - They end the experiment or revise the hypothesis and begin again.

2. How to make a vinaigrette salad dressing
   - Gather the following ingredients: 3–4 tablespoons olive oil, 2 teaspoons Dijon mustard, 1 tablespoon vinegar, salt and pepper to taste.
   - First, combine the mustard and the vinegar. Mix well.

- Next, gradually add the oil, stirring it slowly into the other two ingredients.
- Contrary to popular opinion, olive oil is good for you.
- Finally, add salt and pepper to taste.
- We eat this almost every night.

3. The beating of the human heart
   - The auricles contract, squeezing as much blood into the ventricles as they will hold.
   - The ventricles contract. Pressure of blood within them forces the cuspid valves (which open inward from the auricles) to close and the semilunar valves (which open outward into the arteries) to open.
   - Blood spurts into the arteries.
   - At this point, the beating of the human heart and the beating of the cat heart begin to differ.
   - The ventricles relax and pressure in them falls. Pressure of the blood just pumped into the arteries closes the semilunar valves.
   - Pressure of blood in the auricles opens the cuspid valves, and blood flows into the ventricles.
   - Blood continues to flow into the auricles and on into the ventricles as the entire heart is relaxed and rests briefly.
   - Contraction then begins again.

From *Compton's Interactive Encyclopedia,* 1999, The Learning Company.

Coherence in Process Essays

In process essays, coherence mainly involves the order of information. (To review general information about coherence in essays, see Unit 1, pp. 5–8.)

Maintaining Chronological Order

Writers must present the steps in process essays in the correct, or chronological, order. Chronological order adds coherence to all process essays. It is especially important in instructional process essays, in which the reader should be able to recreate the process that you describe.

EXERCISE 4

Chronological Order

A. *The following essay was written by a "cat lover." The paragraphs in this process essay are not all in the correct order. Number them from 1 to 7 to indicate the best order.*

Cat Bathing as a Martial Art

Many people think that bathing a cat is difficult, but it is really quite easy if you follow a few simple steps.

_____ **A.** First of all, keep in mind that although the cat has the advantage of quickness and lack of concern for human life, you have the advantage of strength. Capitalize on that advantage by selecting the battlefield. Don't try to bathe him in an open area where he can force you to chase him. Pick a very small bathroom with a tightly-closing door.

_____ **B.** Now, it is time to bring in the cat. To do this, use the element of surprise. Pick up your cat nonchalantly, as if to simply carry him to his supper dish. Once you are inside the bathroom, speed is essential for your next move. In a single motion, shut the bathroom door, step into the tub enclosure, dip the cat in the water, and squirt him with shampoo. You have begun the wildest 45 seconds of your life.

_____ **C.** Once your cat has gotten wet and soapy, do not expect to be able to hang on to him for more than a few seconds. He will be slippery and will wiggle free and fall back into the water. This will rinse him off. You can try shampooing him a second time, but check your helmet first and make sure that it is tightly fastened in case he makes a grab for you.

_____ **D.** Once you have chosen the site of the crime, it is time to prepare everything. There will be no time to go out for a towel when you have a cat sinking its claws into your leg. Fill the bathtub with warm water, put the kitty shampoo within easy reach, and dress yourself in heavy protective clothing (I recommend combat boots, a helmet, and heavy overalls) before you begin.

(continued)

(continued)

_____ **E.** In a few days, the cat will relax enough to be removed from your leg. He will usually have nothing to say for about three weeks and will spend a lot of time sitting with his back to you. You will be tempted to assume that he is angry. This isn't usually the case. As a rule he is simply plotting ways to get through your defenses and injure you for life the next time you decide to give him a bath.

_____ **F.** Next, the cat must be dried. Novice cat bathers assume that this part will be the most difficult, for humans generally are worn out by this time. However, drying is actually simple compared to what you have just been through. That's because by now the cat is semi-permanently affixed to your right leg. You simply pop the drain plug with your foot, reach for your towel, and wait. After all the water is drained from the tub, it is a simple matter to reach down and dry the cat.

_____ **G.** At least now he smells a lot better.

Adapted from "Cat Bathing As A Martial Art," by Howard Herron as seen at http://tlcpoodles.tripod.com/catbath.html [May 9, 2002]

B. *Read your reordered essay to a partner. Does your new order make this essay coherent? Does your partner's order? Did you both choose the same order?*

Transition Expressions

***First (second, third, etc.), next, now, then,* and *finally; before, after, once, as soon as,* and *while; during, over, between* + noun phrase**

First (second, third, etc.), next, now, then,* and *finally

Function: *First* signals the first step in a process. *Second, third, next, now,* and *then* signal steps after the first step. *Finally* signals the last step in a process.

Use: These words are adverbs. They usually come at the beginnings of sentences and are followed by a subject and a verb. With the exception of *finally,* they can also be used in the middle or at the end of a sentence to indicate chronological order.

Examples: You should put the egg in the water **first.**

Next, heat the water until it boils.

Finally, remove the pot from the heat and wait fifteen minutes.

(continued)

(continued)

Punctuation note: A comma should follow *first* (*second, third,* etc.), *next, now,* or *finally* when it occurs at the beginning of a sentence. No comma is necessary when it occurs in the middle or at the end of a sentence.

before, after, once, as soon as,* and *while

Function: Signal chronological order to indicate which steps in a process come before, after, or at the same time as others. *Before* signals a step that precedes another step. *After, once,* and *as soon as* signal a step that occurs after another. *As soon as* means *right after. While* is used to describe two steps or stages in a process that happen simultaneously, at the same time.

Use: These words are all subordinating conjunctions which are used in adverb clauses.*

Examples: **After** you put the egg in the water, heat it until it boils.

While the water is heating, peel the vegetables.

Eat the egg and the vegetables **as soon as** they are cooked.

***during, over, between* + noun phrase**

Function: Indicate chronological order. *During* and *over* mean "throughout or inside a time period." *Between* indicates a step that happens within a specific interval or period of time.

Examples: **Over/During** the first few weeks, many changes occur.

Between week 1 and week 3, the plants will grow rapidly.

* See pp. 75–77, Sentence Check, for more information about adverb clauses.

Blueprint Process Essays

In this section, you will read and analyze two sample process essays. These essays can act as blueprints when you write your own process essay in Part B.

Blueprint Process Essay 1: Baby Talk

PREREADING DISCUSSION QUESTIONS

1. *How old is a baby when he or she begins to learn language? How do you know this?*
2. *Do you have any memories about your experience learning your first language? If so, share them with the class.*

EXERCISE 5

Reading and Answering Questions

Read the process essay. Fill in the blanks with transition expressions from the box. Use each expression one time only. Then answer the post-reading discussion questions.

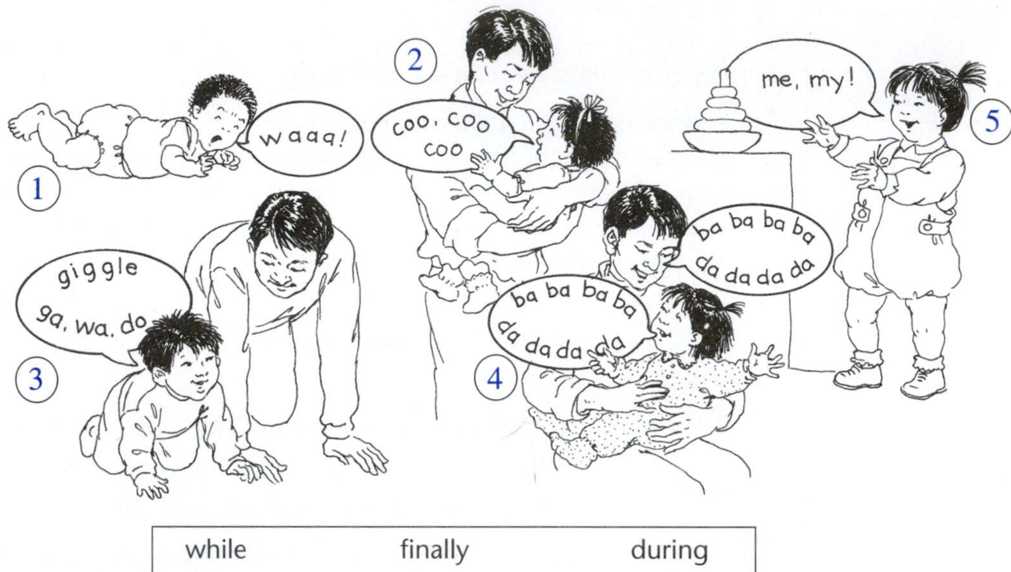

while	finally	during
over	next	before
after	between	

Baby Talk

uttered: spoken

emerge: come out; appear

1. For many parents, a child's first words, **uttered** at around one year of age, mark the first real evidence of language development—the child has "started to talk." However, this ignores a great deal of early progress during the first year, without which no first word would **emerge** at all. This progress is made in several areas, including sound production, speech perception, and speech interaction. Sound production is one of the easiest to recognize and one of the most fascinating. Sound production begins at birth, and by the age of eighteen months, the average child has gone through five unique and important stages of growth in the production of the sounds which eventually open up to her the wonderful world of communication through language.

2. The first stage of sound production, Stage I (0–8 weeks), consists of basic biological noises. ________________ the first few weeks of life, a baby's vocal sounds directly reflect her biological state and activities. States of hunger, pain, or discomfort that cause crying and fussing are common at this stage.

(continued)

cooing: soft and sweet, like the sound of a pigeon

(continued)

3. ______________________, the baby enters Stage II (8–20 weeks). __________________ six and eight weeks, the first **cooing** sounds are produced. These sounds gradually become more frequent and more varied as the child responds to the smiles and speech of adults. Cooing is more musical and quieter than crying. Later in this same period, cooing sounds are strung together—often ten or more at a time. Some of these sequences such as *[ga]* and *[gu]* begin to resemble the syllables of later speech. __________________ the baby is learning to coo, she is also learning to laugh. The first throaty chuckles and laughs emerge at about four months of age.

4. __________________ the baby learns to coo and laugh, she enters Stage III (20–30 weeks). __________________ this stage, vocal play begins. The sounds of vocal play are much steadier and longer than those of cooing. They are also quite varied as the baby begins to experiment with different sound combinations. In addition, there seems to be a strong element of practice in the activities of this period. Anyone who has observed it will also recognize that it usually provides a great deal of enjoyment for parent and child alike as they play together with the sounds of language.

5. __________________ the baby begins to show the signs of using real language, she passes through one more stage—Stage IV (25–50 weeks). This is the babbling stage. Babbling is much less varied than the sounds of vocal play. A smaller set of sounds is used with greater frequency and stability to produce sequences like *[bababa]*, which repeat themselves. Later, this babbling becomes more complex, often including more sounds. Most babbling consists of a small set of sounds very similar to those used in the early language to be spoken by the child.

(continued)

(continued)

vocalization: sound made with the voice

intentions: purposes; meaning

competent: capable; skilled

6. ________________, the child enters Stage V (9–18 months). While babbling continues during this stage, a new **vocalization** also emerges. The Stage V baby begins to produce "proto" words. Parents begin to sense **intentions** behind these utterances, with their more well-defined shape, and often feel they have meaning such as questioning, calling, greeting, or wanting. These are the first real signs of language development, and it is at Stage V that children growing up in different language environments begin to sound increasingly unlike each other.

7. People who do not know about the stages of language development in children often recognize "progress" only at Stage V. How much they are missing! Each stage in a baby's journey to language production is distinct and interesting. Each is important in helping the baby take her "baby steps" toward being a **competent** communicator in her first language.

POSTREADING DISCUSSION QUESTIONS

1. *What kind of process essay is this, instructional or analytical?*

   ____

2. *In the first paragraph, notice the progression of information from general to specific. What introductory technique is the writer using? (See Unit 1, pp. 15–17, for a list of introductory techniques.)*

   ____

3. *Underline the thesis statement. Does it introduce the process that will be discussed in the essay?* ____________________

   What is this process? ____________________

   ____

4. *Just by looking at the thesis statement, how many paragraphs do you think this essay will contain?*

____

5. *Does the entire essay have unity? If not, what should be done to add unity to the essay?*

____

6. *List and label the stages covered in this essay.*

____

7. *Are these stages described in the correct chronological order to make the essay coherent?*

____

8. *Check ✔ the purpose(s) of the conclusion to this essay.*

   ______ *to add coherence to the essay by summarizing or restating the essay subtopics*

   ______ *to add coherence to the essay by restating the essay thesis*

   ______ *to leave the reader with the writer's final thoughts*

   ______ *to make a prediction or suggestion about the topic of the essay*

9. *Does the conclusion sum up the process and discuss its results?*

____

Blueprint Process Essay 2: Exercise for Everyone

PREREADING DISCUSSION QUESTIONS

1. *What is your favorite form of exercise? Why?*
2. *Is there an exercise or fitness activity that you would like to try but never have? If so, what is it?*
3. *If there were a form of exercise that could work well for everyone, what do you think it would be? Why?*

EXERCISE 6

Reading and Answering Questions

Read the classification essay and answer the questions.

Exercise for Everyone

1. Almost everyone today seems interested in being physically fit. Having the flattest "abs" (abdominal muscles), the thinnest thighs, and the loveliest love handles possible has become important for young and old alike. In addition, the methods available for achieving fitness goals are as varied as the people who practice them. You can lift weights, swim, or jog. You can ski, ride horseback, or skate. You can jiggle and joggle your way to fitness through aerobics classes and/or **"spinning"** sessions. If you are interested in competitive activities, you can play tennis, soccer, basketball, or any of a number of other sports. While all of these fitness activities can be highly **beneficial,** each has its **drawbacks** as well. Some cost a lot. Some only exercise parts, not all, of the body. Some demand daily and inconvenient jaunts to a gym. Others require special training, skills, or talents. Still others require special equipment and/or special weather conditions. There is one exercise, however, which provides great overall fitness with minimum investment and maximum convenience. Almost everyone can do it. No lessons are needed, and there are no special fees. No fancy equipment is required, and you can do it almost anywhere or any time you want to. That exercise is walking, and, surprising as it may seem, walking can be the best overall exercise for you if you follow some simple steps to make it effective.

spinning: riding a stationary bicycle with a group of other people and a teacher

beneficial: helpful

drawbacks: disadvantages

2. The first thing you need to do if you want to walk for fitness is to get a good pair of walking shoes. These are the only "special" equipment required by the walker. Any shoes that are comfortable, provide good support, and don't cause **blisters** or **calluses** will do. Light running or hiking shoes with good **arch supports** are popular choices.

3. Next, check your wardrobe. There is no need for you to invest in any special or fancy clothing. Just the basics will do. Generally, loose-fitting clothes that you can layer and unlayer as the temperature goes up and down are all that is needed. A rain poncho or a rain jacket is handy for those who walk in the rain.

blisters: painful swellings of the skin that contain watery liquid

calluses: hard, thick areas of skin, often on the feet

arch supports: special padding to support the middle (arch) of the foot

(continued)

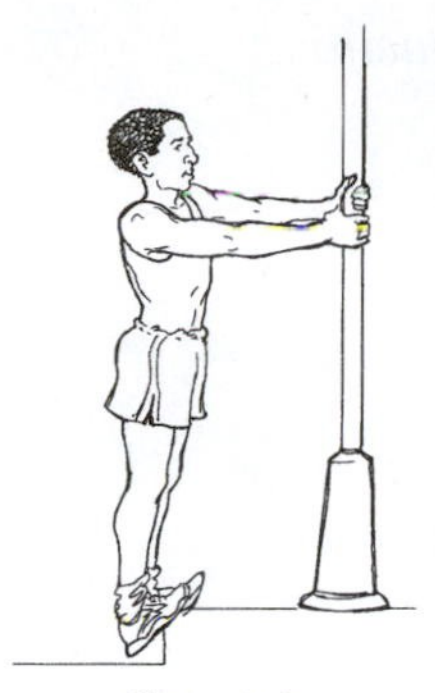
calf stretches

advisable: a good idea; recommended
strides: steps

shin stretches

reach-and-bend stretches

(continued)

4. Once you have good shoes and comfortable clothes, it's time to get started. Before you head out the door, it's a good idea to do a few stretching exercises. These help loosen tight muscles and tone and strengthen your upper body. Some of the most useful pre-walking stretch exercises include calf stretches, shin stretches, and reach-and-bend stretches.

5. After you've stretched, you are ready to start walking. No one can tell you exactly how far or how fast to walk when you first begin, but it is **advisable** to start slowly and gradually lengthen your time and pace. Eventually, your goal should be to comfortably walk three miles in 45 minutes, but there is no hurry about getting there. Just walk as briskly as you can, keeping your head erect, your back straight, and your abdomen flat. Your toes should point straight ahead and your arms should swing loosely at your sides. Take long, easy, **strides,** breathe deeply, and . . . walk!

6. As you near the end of your walk, slow your pace a little at a time. It's important to let your heartbeat return to its normal "resting rate" gradually. In addition, your working muscles will appreciate a gradual return to their less active state.

7. If you follow these simple steps, walking can be your key to overall fitness. This simple, inexpensive exercise, which is based on something that almost all of us do without even thinking about it, can help you reach your fitness goals as effectively as can any other exercise. Take a deep breath, put on those walking shoes, and enjoy! You can really get a good look at the world when it's going by at four miles an hour!

Adapted from: *Walking for Exercise and Pleasure*—
http://www.hoptechno.com/book9/htm and *Walking Wellness On-line*—
http://www.racewalk.com/WWBook/nsp00002.htm June 27, 2001.

POSTREADING DISCUSSION QUESTIONS

1. *What kind of process essay is this, instructional or analytical?*

 ____

2. *Underline the thesis statement. Does it introduce the process that will be discussed in the essay?* ______________

 What is this process? ______________

 ____

3. *Check ✔ the primary technique used in this introduction.*

_______ *the funnel technique*

_______ *posing an interesting question*

_______ *describing a dramatic scene*

_______ *using a relevant quotation*

_______ *turning an argument on its head*

4. *Does this essay lack unity? That is, do any of the steps presented seem irrelevant? If so, which ones?* ______________________________

____

Have any steps been missed? If so, which ones should be added?

____

5. *Does the conclusion successfully signal the end of the essay?*

____

6. *What seem(s) to be the other purpose(s) of the conclusion?*

____

Does it achieve these purposes?

____

Grammar Focus and Sentence Check

In this part of the unit, the first grammar instruction, Grammar Focus, highlights English grammar points that are common problems for ESL students. The second grammar instruction, Sentence Check, will help you write better sentences of different types to include in your essays.

Grammar Focus: Articles

Articles introduce and identify nouns. Articles can be indefinite *(a/an)* or definite *(the).* Articles occur before nouns *(**the** apple)* and before adjective + noun combinations *(**a** large apple).*

IMPORTANT NOTE:

- A noncount noun cannot be preceded by an indefinite article. Instead, *some* or no article (*Ø*) is used.

Incorrect: I need an information.
Correct: I need information.
I need some information.

Incorrect: I enjoy a music.
Correct: I enjoy music.

- Use *a* before consonant sounds. Use *an* before vowel sounds.

Indefinite Articles (*A/An*)

Writers use indefinite articles with singular count nouns (examples: *button, classroom*). Indefinite articles "introduce" singular count nouns into a conversation or a reading. You need to introduce a noun when it is unknown or unspecified to the writer, the reader, or both.

Example: She needs **a** new dress. (no specific dress is known or mentioned) [Article]

Some or no article (*Ø*) can introduce plural count nouns. When no article is used, the noun itself is focused on.

Example: She bought dresses (not shoes) today.

EXERCISE 7

INDEFINITE ARTICLES

Fill in the blank with a, an, *or no article* (Ø).

1. If you want to walk in the rain, you need ______ rain poncho.
2. You will enjoy ______ tennis if you try it.
3. We walked in ______ bad weather last week.
4. I wore ______ old pair of shoes yesterday while I was walking.
5. Now, I have ______ sore foot.
6. I also have ______ uncomfortable blister on my toe.

The Definite Article *(The)*

Writers use *the* with singular, plural, and noncount nouns. *The* is used with a specific or particular noun in these cases:

1. The second time the noun is mentioned.

   Example: I have a cat and a dog. **The cat** is black. **The dog** is white.

2. When the noun is part of or related to something else already introduced.

   Example: I got a new car yesterday. **The** seats are leather.

3. When it is unique, or one of a kind.

   Example: **The sun** was hot today.

4. When it is part of the everyday world of the listener and the speaker.

   Example: Mother to daughter: Could you take out **the trash,** please?

5. When other words in the sentence make the noun specific or known. These words include modifying phrases or clauses.

   Example: **The book** on the table is mine. (*On the table* tells which book.)

6. When the noun is part of a superlative or ranking structure.

   Example: Walking is **the best exercise** for him. **The first time** I walked I didn't enjoy it.

EXERCISE

Definite and Indefinite Articles

Fill in the blanks in these sentences adapted from "Baby Talk" (pp. 66–68). Use a, an, *or* the. *If no article is needed, write* (Ø) *in the blank.*

1. ______ area of sound production is one of ______ easiest areas to recognize and one of ______ most fascinating ones to study.

2. ______ first stage of sound production, Stage I (0–8 weeks), consists of basic biological noises. During ______ first few weeks of life, ______ new baby's vocal sounds directly reflect her biological state and activities.

3. ______ cooing is more musical and quieter than ______ crying.

4. In addition, there seems to be ______ strong element of practice in ______ activities of this period.

5. While ______ babbling continues during this stage, ______ new vocalization also emerges.

Sentence Check: Adverb Clauses

An **adverb clause** is a dependent clause that tells *why, when, where, how,* or *for what purpose* or that introduces an opposite idea. Adverb clauses function like adverbs. They modify the verb or the main clause in a sentence.

Adverb clauses begin with subordinating conjunctions *(because, since, after, as, once, as soon as, while, when, where, wherever, though, although, even though, as if, so that, in order that, whereas).*

Here are some examples of sentences containing adverb clauses. The subordinating conjunctions are in **bold.** The adverb clauses are highlighted.

Adverb clauses telling **why**	He will call her **because** he loves her. **Since** he will always love her, he will not leave her. **As** he will always love her, he cannot leave her.
Adverb clauses telling **when**	**Before** you learn to talk, you learn to babble. **After** you learn to talk, you learn to sing. **Once** you learn to talk, you can express your ideas. **As soon as** you learn to talk, the world is a different place. You continue babbling **while** you are learning to talk. Your world changes **when** you learn to talk.
Adverb clauses telling **where**	They will come and see us **where** we live. We can go **wherever** you want to go.
Adverb clauses telling **how**	He looks **as though** he is happy. She spends money **as if** she were rich!
Adverb clauses telling **for what purpose**	Wear good shoes **so that** you can enjoy your walk. **In order that** you can enjoy your walk, wear good shoes.
Adverb clauses that **introduce an opposite idea**	**Although** I want to go, I can't. **Though** I want to go, I won't. I won't go **even though** I want to. **Whereas** I want to go, he doesn't.

IMPORTANT NOTE:

- Adverb clauses can come at the beginning or at the end of a sentence. When they come at the beginning, put a comma after them. When they come at the end, no comma is usually necessary.

Examples: **When** you want to go, tell me.
Tell me **when** you want to go.

EXERCISE
9

Adverb Clauses Telling When

Because process essays use chronological order, they often include adverb clauses that tell when. Read the sentences from "Exercise for Everyone," pp. 70–71. Fill in the blanks with subordinating conjunctions from this list to form adverb clauses that tell when.

when once before after as

1. Generally, loose-fitting clothes that you can layer and unlayer ____________ the temperature goes up and down are all that is needed.
2. ____________ you have good shoes and comfortable clothes, it's time to get started.
3. ____________ you head out the door, it's a good idea to do a few stretching exercises.
4. ____________ you've stretched, you are ready to start walking.
5. No one can tell you exactly how far or how fast to walk ________ you first begin, but it is advisable to start slowly and gradually lengthen your time and pace.

EXERCISE
10

Sentence Combining to Form Adverb Clauses

Use the subordinating conjunction in parentheses to combine each pair of sentences into one sentence. Write the new sentence, placing the adverb clause in two different orders. Punctuate carefully. The first one is done for you.

1. We don't want to hurt our parents. We love them. (because)

   We don't want to hurt our parents because we love them.

   Because we love our parents, we don't want to hurt them.

2. A baby begins babbling. It is only 25 weeks old. (when)

   ____

   ____

3. Some people enjoy swimming. Other people don't. (whereas)

   ____

   ____

4. He is a very talented artist. He doesn't believe that his art is good. (even though)

____

____

5. He is learning English. He can get a job in England. (so that)

____

____

6. My husband doesn't enjoy going to the theater. We don't see many movies. (since)

____

____

EXERCISE **11**

Editing Practice: Grammar Focus and Sentence Check Application

Read this passage carefully. Find and correct the seven errors with articles and adverb clauses. The first one is done for you.

TOEFL Test Preparation

The Test of English as a Foreign Language (TOEFL) is required for admission to many American colleges and universities. The most effective way to prepare for this test is to work hard to develop overall English language proficiency. In addition, however, there are some test-taking strategies that students can practice when are preparing for the TOEFL. These strategies can help students do well on test, and they include:

1. Use your time wisely. The TOEFL is the timed test.
2. When you aren't sure of the answer to a question, make your best guess.
3. The night before the TOEFL, relax and go to bed early. Although you wake up, you will be fresh and ready for the test.
4. Before you leave home to take the TOEFL, eat a healthy and nutritious food. You will need extra energy when you take this test.

PART B

The Writing Process: Practice Writing a Process Essay

Objectives	**In Part B, you will:**
Prewriting:	practice visualizing, sketching, and listing ideas
Planning:	use a flow chart to organize and sequence ideas
Partner Feedback:	review classmates' sketches and flow charts and analyze feedback
First Draft:	write a process essay
	use the funnel method as an introductory technique
Partner Feedback:	review classmates' essays and analyze feedback
Final Draft:	use feedback to write a final draft of your process essay

The Writing Process: Writing Assignment

Your assignment is to write an instructional process essay that explains the steps for preparing and delivering an effective oral presentation. Follow the steps in the writing process in this section.

Prewriting: Visualizing, Sketching, and Listing

Visualize (imagine a picture of) yourself giving an oral presentation. What are you wearing? How do you feel? Who is your audience? Draw a sketch of yourself and your audience. Include any special tools or equipment that you think you might need in order to do a clear and complete oral presentation, for example, an overhead projector, a computer that projects onto a screen, notecards, etc. What steps would be involved in preparing to give this presentation? List ideas next to your sketch.

Planning: Making a Flow Chart

Now that you have visualized the process involved in preparing and making an oral presentation, the next step is to organize your ideas in chronological order. Using a flow chart is a good way to do this as flow charts capture the importance of chronological order.

Work with the flow chart below. Introduce your process in the first box and also include the general topic. Then fill each large box that flows from this box with a major step that any effective presenter would need to follow (think about what you will do before, during, and after the presentation). In the small boxes to the side, list details and terms that you want to define for general readers—people who may not have much experience giving presentations. Try to include similar details about each step. Use details from your prewriting activity and add more details as you think of them. Write a draft of your thesis statement at the bottom of your chart. You can change it later if you need to.

Here is an example of how your flow chart might be structured:

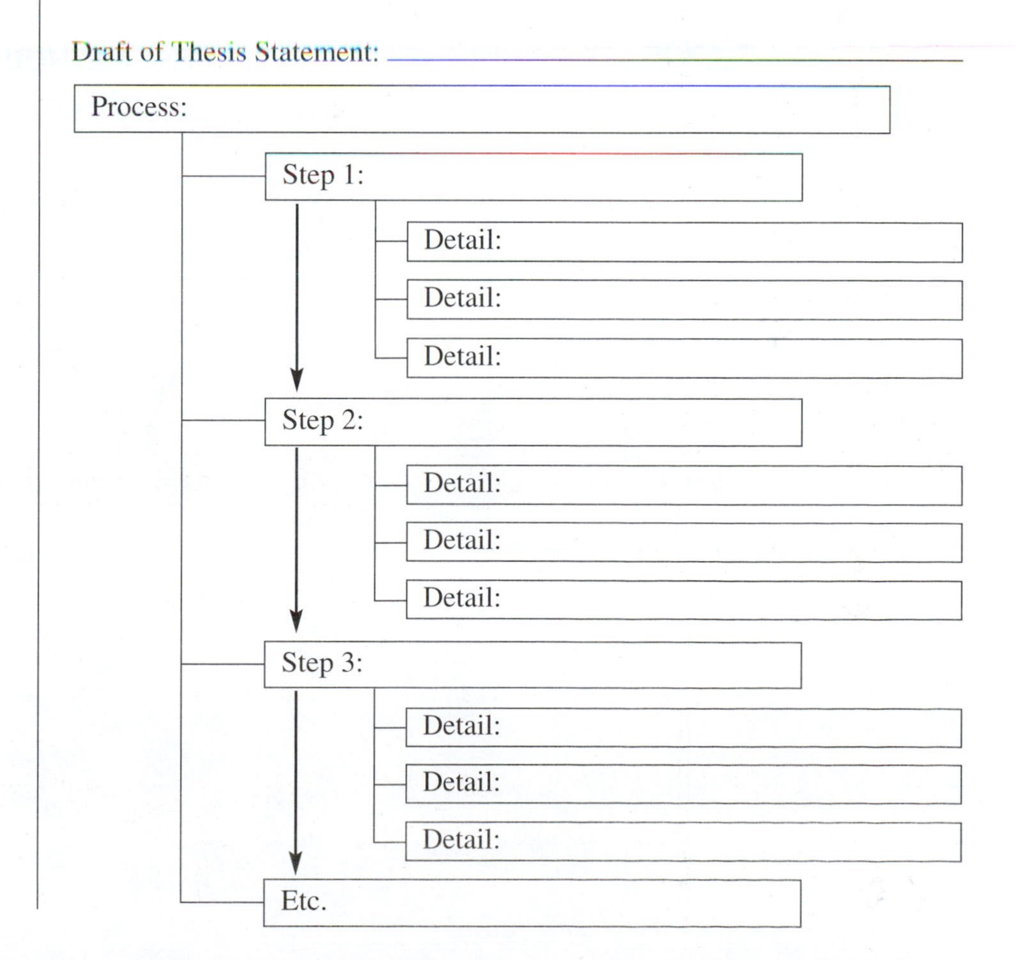

Partner Feedback Form 1

Exchange your sketches from the prewriting activity and your flow chart with another student. Look at your partner's sketches and flow chart and answer the questions on Partner Feedback Form 1: Unit 3, p. 227, in Appendix 3. Discuss your partner's reactions to your sketches and flow chart. Make notes about any parts you need to change before you write your paper. For more information about giving partner feedback, see Appendix 2, p. 218, Guidelines for Partner Feedback.

First Draft

You are now ready to write the first draft of your essay. Before you begin, review your sketches and flowchart and any comments from your partner.

EXERCISE 12

Writing the Introduction

Write an introduction for your essay, using your sketches, your flow chart, and the feedback you received from your partner. To begin your essay, use the funnel technique as explained on p. 15 in Unit 1. Both "Baby Talk" on pp. 66–68 and "Exercise for Everyone" on pp. 70–71 use this introduction technique. You can use them as models if you want. End your introduction with a well-constructed thesis statement. When you finish, use the checklist to review your work.

IMPORTANT NOTE:

Begin your funnel with more general information to give your reader a context for your essay. Gradually focus this information more and more until you reach the "point" of your thesis.

Make sure the information at the "widest" part of your funnel is relevant to your thesis. It should provide background information that is helpful to the reader. It should not present ideas that are not related to the thesis.

FUNNEL METHOD

Introductory Paragraph

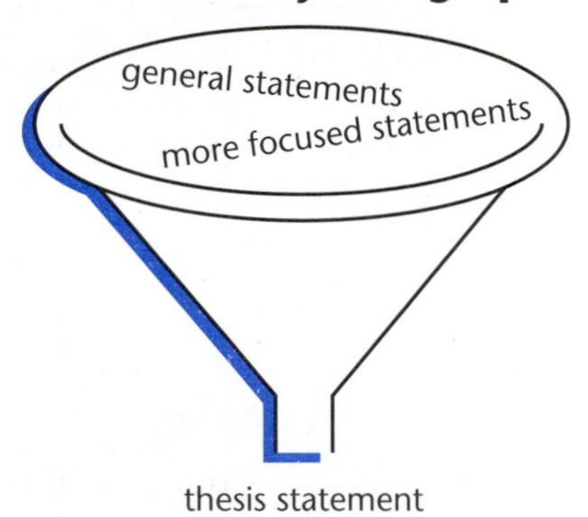

Introduction Checklist

	YES	NO
▸ Did I use the funnel method effectively, moving from general statements to thesis statement?	❑	❑
▸ Does my introduction flow logically from general to more specific?	❑	❑
▸ Does my first paragraph introduce the process?	❑	❑
▸ Does my thesis statement provide the reader with a clear guide for the rest of the essay?	❑	❑
▸ Is the purpose of my essay clear?	❑	❑

What is it? ______________________________

____

____

EXERCISE 13

Writing Body Paragraphs

Look again at your sketches, your flow chart, and your introduction. Then write the body paragraphs. Include any sketches that you think might help a general audience. When you finish, use the checklist to review your work.

Body Paragraph Checklist

	YES	NO
▸ Does each body paragraph in my essay treat only one main idea?	❑	❑
▸ Does each contain a topic sentence with a clear controlling idea?	❑	❑
▸ Does each paragraph end with a logical concluding sentence?	❑	❑
▸ Are all the supporting sentences in my body paragraphs relevant to the topic? That is, do they have unity?	❑	❑
▸ Should I include any sketches in my essay? If so, which ones? ______________________________	❑	❑
▸ Are my body paragraphs arranged in a logical order? That is, do they have coherence?	❑	❑

EXERCISE 14

Writing a Conclusion

Review again your flow chart, introduction, and body. Write a conclusion for your essay. When you finish, use the checklist to review your work.

Conclusion Checklist

	YES	NO
► Does my conclusion successfully signal the end of my essay?	❑	❑
► Does my conclusion add coherence to the essay by:		
a. restating the essay thesis?	❑	❑
b. summarizing or restating the process I described?	❑	❑
► Does my conclusion:		
a. leave the reader with my final thoughts?	❑	❑
b. make a prediction or suggestion about the topic of the essay?	❑	❑

Partner Feedback Form 2

Exchange essays with another student. Read your partner's essay and answer the questions on Partner Feedback Form 2: Unit 3, pp. 229–230, in Appendix 3. Discuss your partner's reactions to your essay. Make notes about any parts you need to change before you write your final draft. For more information about giving partner feedback, see Appendix 2, p. 218, Guidelines for Partner Feedback.

Final Draft

Carefully revise your essay using all the feedback you have received: partner feedback review of your sketches, flow chart and essay, instructor comments, and any evaluation you have done yourself. Use the checklist to do a final check of your essay. In addition, try reading your essay aloud. This can help you find awkward-sounding sentences and errors in punctuation. When you have finished, add a title to your essay, and neatly type your final draft. See Appendix 4, p. 246, for information about writing titles.

Final Draft Checklist

	YES	NO
▸ Did I include a thesis statement that contains a clear topic and controlling idea?	❑	❑
▸ Did I use the funnel method effectively?	❑	❑
▸ Did I completely and clearly explain the process of making and giving an oral presentation?	❑	❑
▸ Did I use transition expressions (*first, second, third,* etc.), *next, now, then,* and *finally; before, after, once, as soon as* and *while; during, over, between* + noun phrase correctly?	❑	❑
▸ Did I use articles and adverb clauses correctly?	❑	❑
▸ Does each of my body paragraphs have a clear topic sentence?	❑	❑
▸ Does my concluding paragraph have clear purposes? What are they? ________________	❑	❑
▸ Does my concluding paragraph successfully signal the end of my essay?	❑	❑
▸ Does my entire essay have unity and coherence?	❑	❑

Additional Writing Assignments from the Academic Disciplines

Beginning with the Prewriting activity on p. 79, use the writing process to write another essay. Choose a topic from the following list.

SUBJECT	*WRITING TASK*
Business	Write an instructional essay about the steps involved in successfully interviewing for a job.
Science	Write an analytical essay in which you explain one of these processes: photosynthesis, how a magnet works, how a tornado forms, how a bee pollinates flowers, or how water is formed from hydrogen and oxygen.
Anthropology	Write an analytical essay that describes the stages of acculturation that a person goes through when moving from his or her country to another country.
Psychology	Write an analytical essay in which you explain the stages in the cognitive development of a child.

UNIT 4

Blueprints for

COMPARISON/CONTRAST ESSAYS

PART A

Blueprints for Comparison/Contrast Essays

Objectives	In Part A, you will:
Analysis:	learn about comparison/contrast essays
Unity and Coherence:	
Unity	learn about using two equivalent topics, including solid supporting points, and creating a clear focus
Coherence: Transition Expressions	learn to use *both* (noun) *and* (noun), *not only . . . but also, nevertheless, on one hand . . . on the other hand, in contrast, whereas, unlike* + noun, *like* + noun, *conversely, although, even though, though*
Grammar Focus:	study comparatives *more, most; -er, -est; as . . . as, the same . . . as*
Sentence Check:	study parallelism
Practice:	practice comparing and contrasting information

What Is a Comparison/Contrast Essay?

Writers use **comparison/contrast essays** when they want to either compare or contrast or to both compare and contrast two (or more) things. Writers can emphasize the similarities, the differences, or both the similarities and differences of the things they are comparing and contrasting.

Three Organizational Methods

When you write a comparison/contrast essay, you can choose one of three organizational methods.

1. comparison only: the writer mainly points out the similarities of the two subjects.
2. contrast only: the writer primarily focuses on the differences between the two subjects.
3. comparison/contrast: the writer discusses both similarities (comparison) and differences (contrast) equally.

In order to plan a comparison/contrast essay, it is important to list the points that you will use to compare or contrast. If there are many more similarities than differences, you might decide to do a comparison essay. If there are many more differences than similarities, you might do a contrast essay. If the number of similarities and differences is about the same, you might find that an essay discussing both similarities and differences is appropriate.

For example, if the topic of your essay is the first two world wars, you could organize a comparison/contrast essay in one of three ways:

1. write about the similarities between the two wars

   COMPARISON

   - similarity: Both began in Europe but spread elsewhere.
   - similarity: Both caused millions of human deaths.
   - similarity: Both resulted in huge shifts in country borders.

2. write about the differences between the two wars

   CONTRAST

   - difference: The two wars began for different reasons.
   - difference: The national leaders in the two wars were very different.
   - difference: The two wars ended differently.

3. discuss both the similarities and the differences equally

   COMPARISON/CONTRAST

   - similarities:

     Both began in Europe but spread elsewhere.

     Both caused millions of human deaths.

     Both resulted in huge shifts in country borders.

   - differences

     The two wars began for different reasons.

     The national leaders in the two wars were very different.

     The two wars ended differently.

EXERCISE 1

Compare/Contrast: Methods of Organization

Read each topic and outline below. Decide whether the method of organization for the essay is comparison, contrast, or comparison/contrast.

1. TOPIC: basketball and tennis

   a. Tennis requires a great deal of stamina, and basketball does, too.

   b. In both sports, there is a great deal of action, and players score numerous points.

   c. Tennis and basketball are popular in countries all over the world.

   METHOD OF ORGANIZATION ______________________

2. TOPIC: the female characters in children's stories and the male characters in children's stories

   a. The male characters usually play the hero roles while the females usually play the helpless roles.

   b. The female characters are usually described in terms of their physical appearance, but the male characters are described in terms of their abilities.

   c. Though female characters often have to make some sort of sacrifice, male characters rarely do.

   METHOD OF ORGANIZATION ______________________

3. TOPIC: Spanish and English

   a. Spanish and English use a similar alphabet. In addition, the basic grammar of the two languages is very similar.

   b. Spanish verb conjugation is much more detailed than that of English. In addition, English nouns have fewer forms than Spanish nouns.

   METHOD OF ORGANIZATION ______________________

4. TOPIC: Switzerland and Bolivia

   a. Neither Switzerland nor Bolivia has a coastline.

   b. Mountains make up a large area of both countries.

   c. The inhabitants of both countries have been relatively isolated over the past few centuries.

   METHOD OF ORGANIZATION ______________________

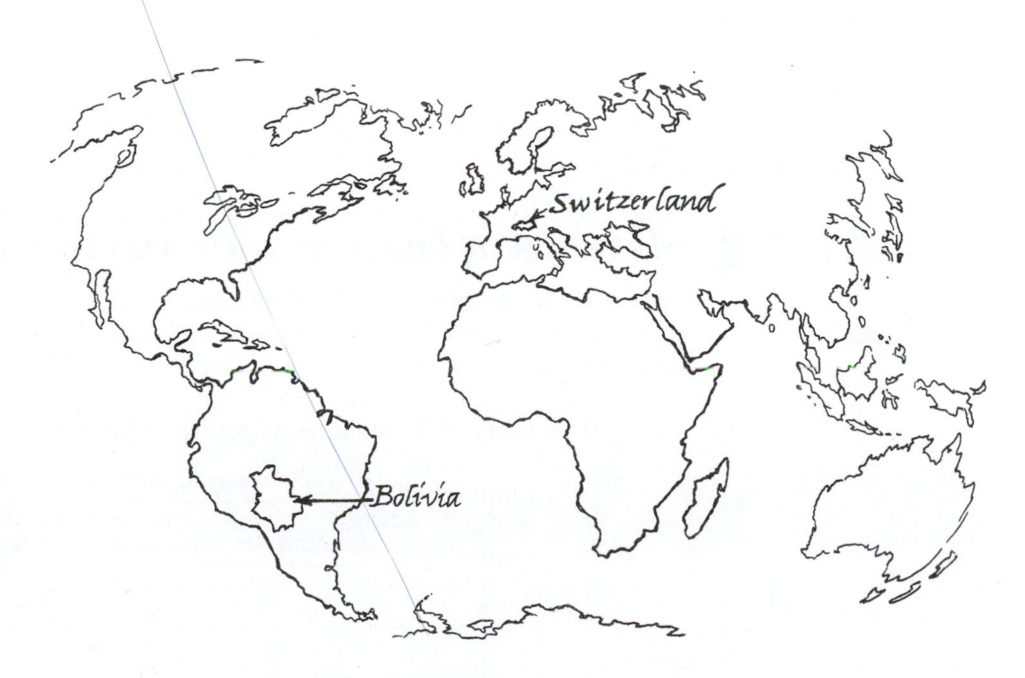

Unity in Comparison/Contrast Essays

At least three things can contribute to better unity in a comparison/contrast essay: 1) using two equivalent topics, 2) including solid supporting points, and 3) creating a clear focus on comparison, contrast, or comparison/contrast.

1. *Using two equivalent topics.* Make sure the things you are comparing belong to the same group. It would be illogical to compare or contrast two items that are not "equivalent." For example, you can compare a movie with another movie or one construction method with another construction method, but you could not logically or fairly compare ocean currents with mountain ranges.

   However, at times, it is not only possible but appropriate to compare two things that on the surface do not appear similar. For example, you might write an essay comparing a famous person with a certain animal, or you might explain how a person's life is like a difficult trip or road. Comparison writing that says A is like B in certain ways is called an *analogy*. An analogy is a more advanced kind of writing plan than a simple comparison or contrast.

2. *Include solid supporting points.* Make a list of the components or parts that you will use to support your comparison or contrast of items. If you are comparing two movies, what points will you use to compare them? In other words, what important components are worth comparing? (Example: plot, setting, characters, actors, acting, director, budget, number of tickets sold, production costs.) If you are comparing two car models, possible components for a comparison/contrast essay include car size, engine size, price, horsepower, gasoline mileage, luxury items, and safety records.

3. *Create a clear focus on comparison, contrast, or comparison/contrast.* All your supporting points should clearly demonstrate that the two topics are similar, different, or both similar and different—depending on your method of organization. Each point must be solid. If even one is weak, unclear, or unrelated, your essay will lose unity.

   See Unit 1, pp. 4–5 and 21–22 for more about unity in essays.

EXERCISE 2

Methods of Organization and Unity

Work with a partner. For each topic and method of organization listed, complete the outlines with appropriate supporting points. The first one is done for you.

1. a. cats as pets and dogs as pets (compare)

   Similarity #1: Most cats and dogs are friendly animals.

   Similarity #2: Caring for cats and dogs is a fairly easy task.

Similarity #3: *Cats and dogs live relatively long lives.*

b. cats as pets and dogs as pets (contrast)

Difference #1: *Dogs like to be petted, but cats are often very aloof.*

Difference #2: *Dogs need to go outdoors often, but cats can live indoors.*

Difference #3: *Dogs do not scratch furniture, but cats do.*

____

2. a. __________ (your native language) and English (compare)

Similarity #1: ______________________________

Similarity #2: ______________________________

Similarity #3: ______________________________

b. __________ (your native language) and English (contrast)

Difference #1: ______________________________

Difference #2: ______________________________

Difference #3: ______________________________

3. a. using the library for sources to write a research paper and using the Internet (compare)

Similarity #1: ______________________________

Similarity #2: ______________________________

Similarity #3: ______________________________

b. using the library for sources to write a research paper and using the Internet (contrast)

Difference #1: ______________________________

Difference #2: ______________________________

Difference #3: ______________________________

EXERCISE 3

Choosing Appropriate Topics and Supporting Information

A. Choose two people and two places to compare and contrast. Then decide on three categories for each that you will use to compare and contrast. For example, for two people, the categories might be personality, looks, and accomplishments. Then fill in details for each category.

Person A and person B (Be sure the two people are "equivalent," i.e., they are both politicians, actors, historical figures, athletes.)

Person A: ______________________________

Person B: ______________________________

CATEGORY	PERSON A INFORMATION	PERSON B INFORMATION
______________	______________	______________
	______________	______________
	______________	______________
	______________	______________
______________	______________	______________
	______________	______________
	______________	______________
	______________	______________
______________	______________	______________
	______________	______________
	______________	______________
	______________	______________

B. Extra Work: Now do the same exercise again but use two places instead of two people. Be sure the two places are "equivalent," i.e., they are both cities, kinds of residences, neighborhoods, countries.

Coherence in Comparison/Contrast Essays

In comparison/contrast essays, transition expressions help create coherence. (To review general information about coherence in essays, see Unit 1, pp. 5–7.)

Transition Expressions

both (noun) *and* (noun), *not only . . . but also . . . , nevertheless, on one hand . . . on the other hand, in contrast, whereas, unlike* + noun, *like* + noun, *conversely, although, even though, though*

***both* (noun) *and* (noun)**

Function: to indicate that two items are included in the information

Use: *Both* (noun) *and* (noun) is a noun phrase. When it is the subject of a sentence, the verb that follows is plural.

Example: **Both mathematics and biology** are required subjects for graduation.

not only . . . but also . . .

Function: to emphasize that both items are included in the information

Use: *Not only* (noun) *but also* (noun) is sometimes a noun phrase. When the noun phrase is the subject of a sentence, the second noun determines whether the verb is singular or plural.

Example: **Not only the electrician but also the carpenters** are working overtime.

Not only (noun) *but also* (noun) can also join two verbs.

Example: He **not only wanted but also needed** her affection. (two verbs)

nevertheless

Function: to indicate that a certain fact will not prevent a second fact from happening

Use: *Nevertheless* is a conjunction that usually occurs at the beginning of a sentence.

Example: The instructor told the students to write exactly five paragraphs in the last essay. Nevertheless, some students wrote essays with only four paragraphs.

Punctuation note: When *nevertheless* occurs at the beginning of a sentence, it is followed by a comma.

on one hand . . . on the other hand

Function: to indicate two contrasting ideas

Use: *On one hand* and *on the other hand* are two phrases that are best used together.

Example: I'm trying to decide whether to buy a new car. **On one hand,** I really need a new car. **On the other hand,** I could save a lot of money by taking the bus or riding my bike for the rest of the summer.

(continued)

(continued)

Punctuation note: Notice that both *on one hand* and *on the other hand* are followed by commas.

in contrast, whereas

Function: to indicate contrast between two items

Use: *In contrast* is an adverbial phrase that usually occurs at the beginning of a sentence. *Whereas* is a conjunction that occurs at the beginning of a clause.

Examples: Traditional banks have very high overhead expenses. **In contrast,** Internet banks do not have the usual kinds of overhead expenses to worry about.

The weather in the summer months is hot and humid, **whereas** the weather in fall is cool and dry.

Punctuation note: *In contrast* is followed by a comma. *Whereas* connects two clauses and is always preceded by a comma.

***unlike* + noun**

Function: to indicate the contrast between two nouns

Use: *Unlike* is a preposition and is always followed by a noun or pronoun.

Example: **Unlike** his father, Elias did not pursue a job in banking.

***like* + noun**

Function: to indicate the similarity between two nouns

Use: *Like* is a preposition and is always followed by a noun or pronoun.

Example: **Like** his father, Elias chose to pursue a job in banking.

conversely

Function: to discuss the opposite situation

Use: *Conversely* is a conjunction that usually occurs at the beginning of a clause.

Example: The trim on this house is white against gray. **Conversely,** the trim on the next house is gray against white.

although, even though, though

Function: to indicate that a certain fact has little effect on a second fact

Use: *Although, even though,* and *though* are subordinating conjunctions. They may be used interchangeably.

Example: **Although (even though, though)** women were important in the development of many kinds of early medicine, they were rarely given credit.

Blueprint Comparison/Contrast Essays

In this section, you will read and analyze two sample comparison/contrast essays. These essays can act as blueprints when you write your own comparison/contrast essay in Part B.

Blueprint Comparison/Contrast Essay 1: Examining the Popularity of Julia Roberts' Characters

PREREADING DISCUSSION QUESTIONS

1. *Here is a partial list of films that actress Julia Roberts starred in. Which of these films have you seen? What was Julia Roberts' role in these movies?*

   a. Pretty Woman

   b. Erin Brockovich

   c. My Best Friend's Wedding

   d. ______________________ (Add another Julia Roberts film that you have seen.)

2. *Do you see any similarities in the characters that Roberts usually plays? If so, what are they?*

EXERCISE 

Reading and Answering Questions

Read the comparison/contrast essay. Fill in the blanks with transition expressions listed here. Then answer the postreading questions.

like	although	however
not only . . . but also		both . . . and

Examining the Popularity of Julia Roberts' Characters

1 According to actress Julia Roberts, "What's nice about my dating life is that I don't have to leave my house. All I have to do is read the paper: I'm marrying Richard Gere, dating Daniel Day-Lewis . . . and even Robert De Niro was in there for a day." What makes Roberts such a popular person in both regular and gossip papers is the type of movie character that she plays. The public loves her characters and her acting. Two of the

(continued)

(continued)

acclaimed: praised

broke: out of money

most widely **acclaimed** movies in which she has starred are *Pretty Woman* and *Erin Brockovich.* In *Pretty Woman,* which was released in 1990, Roberts plays the role of Vivian Ward, a Hollywood Boulevard prostitute who meets and falls in love with Edward, a handsome and rich businessman. In the 1998 release of *Erin Brockovich,* Roberts plays the real-life role of Erin Brockovich, a **broke,** out-of-work single mother who lands a clerical job at a law firm where she ends up fighting a long legal battle against a large power company that is responsible for the deaths and illnesses of several people. Although Vivian and Erin are two very different roles, these two characters are actually similar in at least three important ways.

impoverished: extremely poor

integral: main, major

2 First of all, both Vivian and Erin are poor. Vivian is a prostitute without much money. When Edward takes care of her for several days, it is the first time that she has stayed in such a nice hotel and eaten in elegant restaurants. Similarly, Erin is broke. She has lost her job and is desperately looking for employment because she has to take care of not only herself but also her children. Clearly, the **impoverished** conditions that these two characters face form an **integral** part of who they are and why they act as they do in the stories.

underdog: a person who is not favored to win a competition

insurmountable: unable to overcome or resolve

3 In addition to the fact that they are both poor, Vivian and Erin are also both **underdogs.** They have each faced difficulties that seemed **insurmountable.** Through hard work and some well-timed luck, however, they are able to overcome their problems. Vivian's problem

(continued)

continued

involves her love for someone who is unlikely to return her affections. Vivian makes the mistake of falling in love with one of her clients, Edward, who is extremely rich and belongs to another social class. Nevertheless, he also falls in love with Vivian. In the end, Vivian is able to realize her dream of a better life. Erin, ________________, faces a difficult battle as she confronts a huge corporation that has been accused of polluting a land area and harming people. Through hard work, determination, and some luck, Erin is eventually able to defeat the corporation. Neither character at first seems likely to be able to succeed against the difficult circumstances that she faces.

4 Finally, both characters are able to maintain a certain level of grace despite the awful problems that they face. Vivian gives helpful advice to her best friend, who is also a prostitute with even less chance of escaping her street job. ________________ Vivian, Erin has reached bottom. She is a mother with absolutely no money to feed her children. She has nowhere to turn for help. Throughout all of this, ________________, we never get the sense that Erin has given up or lost hope. She does everything possible to find a job that might help get her family out of trouble. For many audience members, one of the truly appealing aspects of both characters is the fact that they are able to keep their spirits high even though life has **thrown them some real curves.**

throw (someone) a curve: give someone a difficult challenge (the term comes from a curve ball in baseball, which is one of the most difficult balls to hit)

5 Though Vivian in *Pretty Woman* as a prostitute and Erin in *Erin Brockovich* as an out-of-work mother might not seem so similar at first glance, a closer look at these two characters reveals that they are similar in

(continued)

(continued)

at least three important ways. First of all, both Vivian and Erin are poor, a fact that motivates their actions to some degree. ________________, Vivian and Erin are underdogs who are able to overcome tremendous obstacles to reach their goals. Finally, both characters are able to accomplish all of this while maintaining a certain level of grace. Despite the differences in these characters, perhaps it is their similarities that have attracted so many millions of moviegoers to *Pretty Woman* and *Erin Brockovich.*

POSTREADING DISCUSSION QUESTIONS

1. *What is the thesis statement of this essay? Write it here.*

   ____

   ____

2. *Is the writer comparing or contrasting?* ________________

3. *What is being compared or contrasted?* ________________

   ____

4. *Complete this list of paragraph topics:*

   Paragraph 1: introduction

   Paragraph 2: the poverty of both characters

   Paragraph 3: ________________________________

   Paragraph 4: ________________________________

   Paragraph 5: conclusion

5. *Unity: A good writer can achieve unity by providing appropriate supporting details. In paragraph 4, what examples of problems and grace does the writer give for each character?*

	EXAMPLES OF PROBLEMS:	***EXAMPLES OF GRACE:***
Vivian:	________________	________________
Erin:	________________	________________

6. *Does the conclusion offer a suggestion, opinion, or prediction?*

____

Write it here in your own words. ______________________________

____

Blueprint Comparison/Contrast Essay 2: **Two Kinds of English**

PREREADING DISCUSSION QUESTIONS

1. *Have you studied mostly American English or British English? Why?*
2. *In what ways are American English and British English different?*
3. *Can you write a sentence that would have a very different meaning for a speaker of American English than it would for a speaker of British English?*

EXERCISE 5

Reading and Answering Questions

Read the comparison/contrast essay and answer the questions.

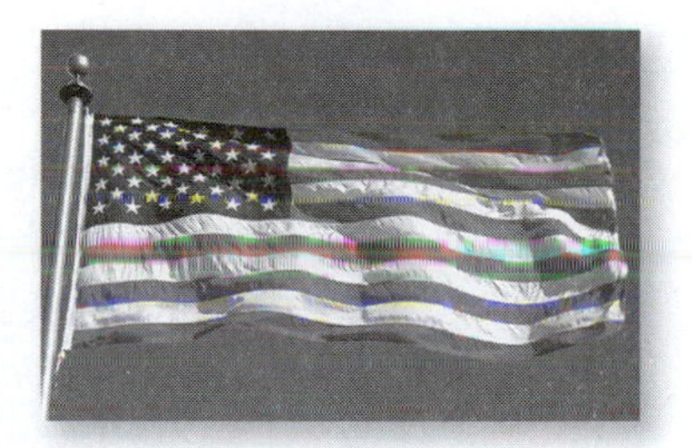

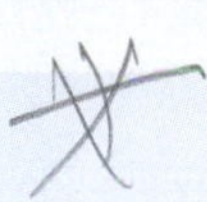

Two Kinds of English

1 Most of us are familiar with the song lyrics "You say poTAYto and I say poTAHto, you say toMAYto and I say toMAHto." These lyrics exemplify one of the differences between American and British English, the two most widely spoken varieties of global English. Despite the **seemingly** endless number of similarities between the two, significant differences between American English and British English in three specific linguistic areas make each one quite **distinct** from the other.

seemingly: apparently

distinct: different

2 Pronunciation is perhaps the first difference that people notice between American and British English. Some individual sounds are consistently different. For example, PoTAYto in American English comes out as poTAHto in British English. WateR in American English is pronounced as wateH in British English. TUna in American English comes out as TYUna in British English. Furthermore, certain whole words are pronounced quite differently. *Schedule* is pronounced with a "k" sound in

(continued)

(continued)

American English but with a "sh" sound, as *shedule,* in British English. The stress in the word *aluminum* in American English is on the second syllable, so it is pronounced aLUminum by Americans. Stress in this same word in British English is on the third syllable, so British English speakers pronounce it aluMInum. These pronunciation differences, though noticeable, do not **impede** real communication. In addition, neither American English nor British English has a better pronunciation than the other; they are simply different.

impede: limit, cause difficulties for

3 A second difference is in spelling. One example of this is the spelling of the vowels preceding the letter *r* in certain words. Americans write *color* and *endeavor.* In British English, however, these same words would be written *coloUr* and *endeavoUr.* Another obvious spelling difference is in the final syllable in words that finish in –er in American English and –re in British English. Examples of this include *centER* in American English with *centRE* in British English. Another common example is *theatER* versus *theatRE.*

4 Finally, perhaps the most **striking** difference between American and British English is vocabulary. For whatever reason, people **tend to** notice vocabulary much more than they do pronunciation or spelling. Some words exist in American English but not in British English, and vice-versa. For example, *traffic circle* and *windshield* are American English words while *mackintosh* (raincoat) and *queue* (a line of people) are British English words. In addition, there are words that exist in both varieties of English, but they have totally different meanings. For example, in British English *biscuits* are sweet (American English translation: cookies), but biscuits in American English are small, salty rounds of bread. In British English, a *bonnet* is the trunk of a car, while in American English, a *bonnet* is a kind of women's hat.

striking: bold, clearly seen

tend to + verb: usually do (a certain action)

5 All languages have local dialects or regional variations, but for historical, geographical, and perhaps political reasons, English has two influential varieties: American English and British English. These varieties are different, yet they are similar enough that the differences that do exist in pronunciation, spelling, and vocabulary rarely **hinder** communication. With modern technology making the world a smaller place, it is likely that these two varieties of English will gradually lose most of their unique characteristics and therefore become more similar.

hinder: hurt, limit, cause difficulties for

POSTREADING DISCUSSION QUESTIONS

1. *What is the thesis statement of this essay? Write it here*

   ____

   ____

2. *How many subtopics are there? What are they?*

   ____

   ____

3. *Is this a comparison, contrast, or comparison/contrast essay?*

   ____

4. *Complete this list of paragraph topics.*

   Paragraph 1: ______________________________________

   Paragraph 2: ______________________________________

   Paragraph 3: ______________________________________

   Paragraph 4: ______________________________________

   Paragraph 5: ______________________________________

5. *Hook. Write the quotation that this essay begins with.*

   ____

   ____

   Explain how this quote is related to the content of this essay.

   ____

   ____

6. *Unity. A good writer can achieve unity by providing appropriate supporting details. Reread the supporting details in paragraph 4 about the two kinds of vocabulary differences between American English and British English. What are the two types of differences and what examples does the author use to support them?*

   Difference #1: ______________________________________

   Examples of #1: ______________________________________

   ____

   ____

   Difference #2: ______________________________________

   Examples of #2: ______________________________________

   ____

   ____

7. *Does the conclusion offer a suggestion, opinion, or prediction?*

____

Write it here in your own words.

____

____

Grammar Focus and Sentence Check

In this part of the unit, the first grammar instruction, Grammar Focus, highlights English grammar points that are common problems for ESL students. The second grammar instruction, Sentence Check, will help you write better sentences of different types to include in your essays.

Grammar Focus: Making comparisons with **more, most; -er, -est; as . . . as, the same . . . as**

In comparison/contrast writing, you need to know how to correctly construct a comparison of two (or more) items. Here are a few guidelines for forming comparison structures in English.

When items are not equal

Comparatives (formed with *-er . . . /more/less*) are used to talk about two things that are different. Superlatives (formed with *-est . . . /most/least*) talk about three or more things that are different.

1. Add *–er* or *–est* to an adjective or an adverb that has only one syllable or that has two syllables but ends in the letter *–y.*

		comparative	superlative
Examples:	clean:	cleaner	cleanest
	happy:	happier	happiest (change the *y* to *i*)

2. Add the word *more/most* or *less/least* in front of all adjectives of two syllables that do not end in *–y,* in front of any adjective with more than two syllables, and in front of adverbs ending in *–ly.*

   Examples: *stubborn:* more stubborn/the most stubborn/ less stubborn/the least stubborn

   successful: more successful/the most successful/ less successful/the least successful

   simply: more simply/the most simply/less simply/the least simply

3. Often the comparative is followed by *than.*

   Example: This restaurant is cleaner **than** the other one.

IMPORTANT NOTE:

Some adjectives are exceptions to the rules for forming regular comparatives. Study these examples:

	Comparative	Superlative
bad	worse	the worst
good	better	the best
little	less	the least

When items are equal

There are two constructions you can use to indicate that two items are either similar or the same.

1. With an adjective or adverb, use *as . . . as.*

   Examples: as generous as (adjective)
   as suddenly as (adverb)

2. With a noun, use *the same . . . as* when you want to say that the two items are equal.

   Example: the same data as

Here is a summary of the rules for forming comparisons, with some examples:

Adjective or adverb	Comparative	Superlative *
1 syllable	taller (than)	the tallest
2 syllables, ending in *–y*	lazier (than) friendlier (than)	the laziest the friendliest
2 syllables, not ending in *–y*	more modern (than)	the most modern
Adverbs ending in *–ly*	more quickly (than)	the most quickly
3 or more syllables	more intelligent (than)	the most intelligent *Note the article *the* in front of superlatives.

Word	Equality for adjective/adverb	Equality for noun
any length word	as tall as	the same height as
	as important as	the same importance as
	as green as	the same color as
	as quickly as	the same speed as

EXERCISE

COMPARISONS IN *TWO KINDS OF ENGLISH*

Find three examples of comparative and superlative forms in Two Kinds of English *on pp. 97–98. Write an example on each blank and then write the rule it follows.*

1. Comparative or superlative: ______________________________

   Rule: ______________________________

2. Comparative or superlative: ______________________________

   Rule: ______________________________

3. Comparative or superlative: ______________________________

   Rule: ______________________________

EXERCISE 7

Comparative and Superlative Forms

Fill in the blank with the correct form of the adjective or adverb in parentheses. You may need to add other words to complete the comparison. Use more, -er, most *or* -est *when you see a plus sign (+). Use* less *or* least *when you see a minus sign (–). Use the same when you see an equal sign (=).*

1. Some people who have studied French and Spanish believe that French grammar is (+difficult) ________________ than Spanish grammar. However, many nonnative speakers believe that English grammar is (+hard) ________________.
2. There is very little difference in the price of these two shirts. In fact, this shirt is almost (=price) ________________ that one.
3. Susan is (+old) ________________ of seven children.
4. What was (+important) ________________ decision that you have ever had to make?
5. I need to know if the inseam on these pants is (=long) ________________ the inseam on those pants.
6. Regular fried chicken is (-spicy) ________________ curried chicken.

IMPORTANT NOTE:

Items in parallel structure are items in a series and must be separated by commas. *Use commas only if there are three or more items.

Examples:

Jenny and Michele really enjoy swimming, running, and skiing.

Jenny, Michele, and Paula really enjoy *swimming and running.*

*When there are three or more items in a series, some punctuation guides say that the comma before the connector word (usually *and*) is optional. However, we encourage writers to use a comma to separate all items in a list of three or more.

Possible: She studied history, biology and art.

Better: She studied history, biology, and art.

Sentence Check: Parallelism

Parallelism, or parallel structure, in sentences means that all of the components in a series have the same grammatical structure. Here are some examples of parallel structure.

verbs:
She **turned on** the machine, **put** the container inside, and **waited** patiently for the next seven minutes.

two past participles:
The manuscript was **written** in 1965 and **published** as a book in 1971.

three objects of the preposition in:
To promote its latest product, the company is interested in **placing** ads in local newspapers, **distributing** flyers to people's homes, and perhaps **running** a commercial on local TV.

EXERCISE

Punctuation with Parallelism

Put boxes around the parallel items. Add commas to the items in parallel structure where needed. Then on the blank, identify the types of parallel structure. The first one has been done for you.

1. The best beaches in the world are located in Thailand in Southeast Asia, Florida in the Southeast U.S., and Nice in southern France.

   noun (prepositional phrase) + noun (prepositional phrase) + noun (prepositional phrase)

2. The menu posted near the door indicates that the restaurant serves fried baked boiled or stuffed shrimp.

   ____

3. Designed by Pierre Boden created by Michele Auger and mass-produced at a factory in China, the new doll has proved to be an instant success.

   ____

4. As a teacher at that school, Mrs. Erwin's tasks include grading student reports summarizing test results and writing student evaluations.

____

EXERCISE

Practice with Parallelism

Fill in the blanks with any word that is appropriate for the meaning of the sentence. Be sure that you maintain parallel structure. The first one is done for you.

1. In addition to collecting stamps, my three favorite hobbies are watching TV, fixing cars, and listening to music.
2. During the middle of the night, a thief broke into the house and ____.
3. Every learner should invest in a good dictionary because having an extensive vocabulary is important to do well on tests, to read more efficiently, and ____.
4. There are wonderful beverages to drink and _______________, so please help yourself.
5. Once the movie ended, the employees _______________, swept the floors, and then washed the seat arms.

EXERCISE

10

Parallel Structures from Blueprint Essays

Look at these sentences taken from the Blueprint essays in this unit. Each contains a parallel structure. Put a box around the parallel structures and identify what kind they are. The first one is done for you.

A. From *Examining the Popularity of Julia Roberts' Characters*

1. This is the first time that she has stayed in a nice hotel and eaten in elegant restaurants.

   These are two past participles. This is the present perfect tense. It also includes a prepositional phrase.

2. Through hard work, determination, and some luck, Erin is eventually able to defeat the corporation.

   ____

   ____

3. Though Vivian in *Pretty Woman* as a forlorn prostitute and Erin in *Erin Brockovich* as an out-of-work mother might not seem so similar at first glance, a closer look at these two characters reveals that they were similar in at least three important ways

____

____

B. From *Two Kinds of English*

1. Examples of this include *color/colour* and *endeavor/endeavour.*

____

____

2. For whatever reason, people tend to notice vocabulary much more than they do pronunciation or spelling.

____

____

3. Pronunciation variations are perhaps the first difference that people notice between American and British English.

____

____

EXERCISE 11

Editing Practice: Grammar Focus and Sentence Check Application

Read these paragraphs carefully. Find and correct the nine errors in comparative forms and parallelism. The first one is done for you.

A quick glance at the locations of Switzerland in central Europe and Bolivia in South America indicates to us that these countries are probably different in a number of ways, but many interesting similarities exist between these two countries, too. The comparisons include size, terrain, ~~the people speak more than one language,~~ *language* and location.

One difference is in size. Bolivia is much large than Switzerland. In fact, Bolivia is about twenty-five times bigger than Switzerland's size.

(continued)

(continued)

Another difference is in the standard of living. Switzerland has a more high standard of living, including better health care. The infant mortality rate in Switzerland is thirteen times less than Bolivia. Although Switzerland is known around the globe for its high mountains, a surprising difference might be that Bolivia has higher mountains than those in Switzerland. In fact, Switzerland has the high mountains in Europe, but the highest mountain in Bolivia is about two thousand meters higher than the highest mountain in Switzerland. Another interesting similarity is that both countries have multiple official languages, so many people speak more that one language. Finally, both countries are landlocked, and both countries have a same number of bordering countries. Though many people expect these two countries to have many important differences, most are surprised that there are so many similarities between Switzerland and Bolivia.

PART B

The Writing Process: Practice Writing a Comparison/Contrast Essay

Objectives	In Part B, you will:
Prewriting:	use a list to generate categories for comparison/contrast
Planning:	use a T-diagram to organize and then sequence ideas for comparison/contrast
Partner Feedback:	review classmates' T-diagrams and analyze feedback
First Draft:	write a comparison/contrast essay
	use a quotation as an introductory technique
Partner Feedback:	review classmates' essays and analyze feedback
Final Draft:	use feedback to write a final draft of your comparison/contrast essay

The Writing Process: Writing Assignment

Your assignment is to write a comparison/contrast essay about two places. The example given here is of Texas and Alaska, but choose any two places you want. Follow the steps in the writing process in this section.

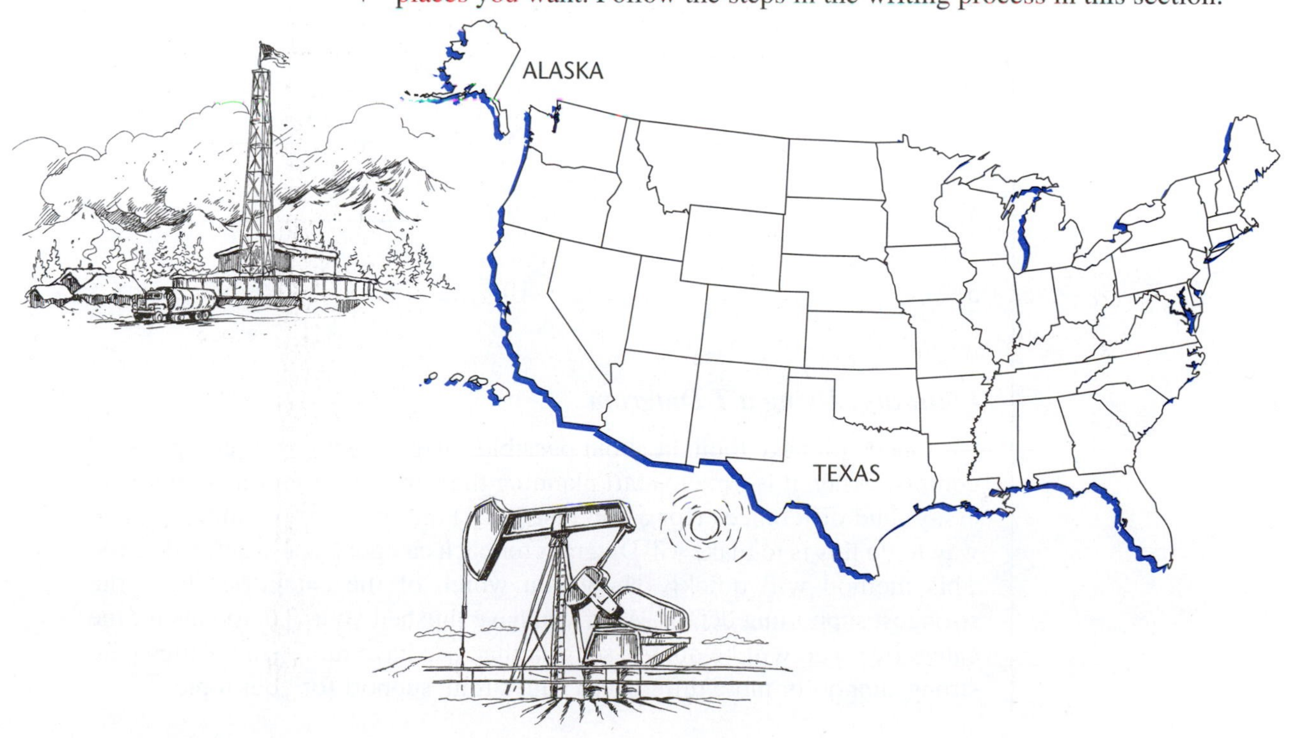

Prewriting: Using Lists to Generate Categories for Comparison/Contrast

One important thing to do before writing a comparison/contrast essay is to make a list of general categories for comparing or contrasting two equivalent things. For example, if you were to write a comparison/contrast essay about two former U.S. presidents, Abraham Lincoln and John F. Kennedy, your list might include some of these categories:

dates when in office	physical characteristics
accomplishments in office	problems faced as president
family life	overall political careers
education and professional training	military experience
intelligence	death (assassination)

EXERCISE 12

Categories for Comparison/Contrast within an Essay

What two places will you compare or contrast in your essay? Write the names of the two places here:

_______________ *and* _______________.

Now consider these two places as you list ten categories that you think could be useful in writing a comparison/contrast essay about your two places. The first one is suggested for you. (Remember that your final essay will not use all ten categories. At this point, you are brainstorming to come up with as many potential categories for comparison/contrast as possible.)

1. size	6. ____________
2. ____________	7. ____________
3. ____________	8. ____________
4. ____________	9. ____________
5. ____________	10. ____________

Planning: Using a T-Diagram

Once you have thought about possible categories for your comparison/contrast essay, it is time to start planning the similarities (for a comparison essay) and differences (for a contrast essay) that you will include. A good way to do this is to make a T-Diagram for each category you want to discuss. This method will quickly show you which of the categories have the strongest supporting details. After you have finished your T-diagrams for the categories, you will be able to see whether you have more similarities with strong support or more differences with strong support for your topic.

Study Sample T-Diagrams

You can make a T-Diagram that looks like the ones below. Note that on the horizontal line, you write the category for comparison or contrast. To the left of the vertical line, write one of the places you are comparing (example: Texas). Below this, list appropriate details for that place. Do the same thing to the right of the vertical line for the other place you are comparing (example: Alaska).

For example, to compare and contrast Alaska and Texas, one possible category is *location*. Here is what a T-Diagram for *location* for Alaska and Texas might look like:

location	
Alaska	Texas
NW corner	south central
near Canada	near Mexico

It is easy to see that the location of these two states is different. Therefore, this category and its supporting ideas would be for a *contrast* point.

Another possible category is *natural resources*. Study this T-diagram for Alaska and Texas:

natural resources	
Alaska	Texas
oil (25% of U.S. supply)	oil
	fishing
fishing	farming
natural gas	natural gas

Without looking at the facts carefully, people might think that the natural resources of these two states would be very different because these states are so far apart geographically. However, when we look at the list in the T-Diagram, we can see that there are many more similarities than differences. Therefore, this category and its supporting information might be useful for a *comparison* point.

EXERCISE 13

Expanding Categories with T-Diagrams

Review the categories that you came up with in Exercise 12. Choose what you think are the five strongest categories and fill in these blank T-diagrams with information related to each of those categories. If necessary, consult a reference source (for example, Internet or encyclopedia) to find good supporting information. When you have finished everything, circle what you consider to be the three T-diagrams that offer the best information for forming a comparison/contrast essay about the two places you chose.

place 1	place 2

place 1	place 2

place 1	place 2

place 1	place 2

place 1	place 2

Using T-Diagram Information to Formulate a Thesis Statement

Look at the information in your T-Diagrams in Exercise 13. Decide whether each T-Diagram is a point for comparison or for contrast.

Next, decide whether you will write a comparison essay, a contrast essay, or a comparison/contrast essay. Remember that this decision is based on where you have the most supporting information. If you have more details for comparison, you will write a comparison essay. If you have more details for contrast, you will write a contrast essay. If your information is about evenly split, then you will write a comparison/contrast essay. You may want to review these three organizational methods on pp. 85–86.

One student writing an essay on Alaska and Texas decided that she had more comparison T-diagrams than contrast T-diagrams. She decided that her best supporting information was in the areas of history, climate, and natural resources. Based on this, she wrote the following thesis statement for her essay:

Though far apart on the map, Alaska and Texas have similarities in history, extreme climates, and natural resources.

This thesis statement is clear. Because the key word is "similarities," we know that she will write a comparison essay about the two states. In addition, we know that the first body paragraph will talk about the history of the two states, the next one will talk about their climates, and the next about their natural resources.

EXERCISE 14

Writing a Thesis Statement from the T-Diagrams

Decide if you have enough supporting details for a comparison, contrast, or comparison/contrast essay. Based on this information, write a thesis statement for your essay.

Draft of Thesis Statement:

___

___

Partner Feedback Form 1

Exchange T-diagrams with another student. Read your partner's T-diagrams and answer the questions on Partner Feedback Form 1: Unit 4, p. 231, in Appendix 3. Discuss your partner's reactions to your T-diagrams. Make notes about any parts you need to change before you write your paper. For more information about giving partner feedback, see Appendix 2, p. 218, Guidelines for Partner Feedback.

First Draft

You are now ready to write the first draft of your essay. Before you begin, review your T-diagrams and any comments from your partner.

EXERCISE 15

Writing the Introduction

Write an introduction for your essay, using your T-diagrams and the feedback you received from your partner. In your introduction, use the "using a relevant quotation" *technique as explained on p. 16, Unit 1.*

Using a quotation to open an essay works well as a hook to draw the reader into the essay. Readers are interested in what others have already said about a topic. Using a good quotation from a well-known person will increase reader interest in your essay immediately.

Both "Examining the Popularity of Julia Roberts' Characters" *on pp. 93–96 and* "Two Kinds of English" *on pp. 97–98 use the relevant quotation technique. You can use them as models if you want.*

Reread the opening quote for "Examining the Popularity of Julia Roberts' Characters" *on p. 93. Then read the next two sentences that connect to*

IMPORTANT NOTE:

Here are some tips for using relevant quotes:

- After the quotation, immediately connect its content to the background information and thesis statement that are coming.
- Select an interesting quotation—something that will take your reader by surprise or that you think he or she will want to know more about.
- Keep the quotation short. Long quotations will lose your reader's attention and disrupt the flow of ideas.
- Choose a quotation from a person or organization that all your readers can recognize. The more your readers can connect with the person, the more they will connect with you and your essay.
- If the quoted person or organization is well-known, be sure to mention the name. If the name is not well known, do not mention it. Instead, use a more general identification such as "a well-known actor recently said . . ." or consider omitting the name altogether.

background information and the thesis statement. Can you see how the information in the quote is related to the essay's topic?

End your introduction with a well-constructed thesis statement. When you finish, use the checklist to review your work.

Introduction Checklist

	YES	NO
► Did I use an effective quotation to hook my audience?	❑	❑
► Is the author of the quote identified?	❑	❑
► Is the author of the quote well-known by the readers?	❑	❑
► Does my introduction flow logically from more general to more specific?	❑	❑
► Does my thesis statement provide the reader with a clear guide for the rest of the essay?	❑	❑
► Is the purpose of my essay clear? What is it?	❑	❑

EXERCISE 16

Writing Body Paragraphs

Look again at your T-diagrams and at your introduction. Then write the body paragraphs. When you finish, use the checklist to review your work.

Body Paragraph Checklist

	YES	NO
▸ Does each body paragraph in my essay treat only one main idea?	❑	❑
▸ Does each contain a topic sentence with a clear controlling idea?	❑	❑
▸ Is it clear whether the paragraph is discussing mainly similarities (comparing) or mainly differences (contrasting)? Or is it discussing similarities and differences?	❑	❑
▸ Does each paragraph end with a logical concluding sentence?	❑	❑
▸ Do my body paragraphs all relate to and support the thesis statement of the essay?	❑	❑
▸ Are my body paragraphs arranged in a logical order? For many writers, this means moving from weakest to strongest support. Conversely, some writers prefer to start with the strongest support and finish with the weakest support.	❑	❑
▸ Are all the supporting sentences in my body paragraphs relevant to the topic? That is, do they have unity?	❑	❑

EXERCISE

17

Writing a Conclusion

Review again your T-diagrams, partner feedback form, introduction, and body. Write a conclusion for your essay. When you finish, use the checklist to review your work.

Conclusion Checklist

	YES	NO
▸ Does my conclusion successfully signal the end of my essay?	❑	❑
▸ Does my conclusion add coherence to the essay by:		
a. restating the essay thesis?	❑	❑
b. summarizing or restating the topics being compared and/or contrasted?	❑	❑
▸ Does my conclusion:		
a. leave the reader with my final thoughts?	❑	❑
b. offer a suggestion, an opinion, or a prediction about the topic of the essay?	❑	❑

Partner Feedback Form 2

Exchange essays with another student. Read your partner's essay and answer the questions on Partner Feedback Form 2: Unit 4, pp. 233–234, in Appendix 3. Discuss your partner's reactions to your essay. Make notes about any parts you need to change before you write your second draft. For more information about giving partner feedback, see Appendix 2, p. 218, Guidelines for Partner Feedback.

Final Draft

Carefully revise your essay using all the feedback you have received: partner feedback review of your T-diagrams and essay, instructor comments, and any evaluation you have done yourself. Use the checklist to do a final check of your essay. In addition, try reading your essay aloud. This can help you find awkward-sounding sentences and errors in punctuation. When you finish, add a title to your essay, and neatly type your final draft. See Appendix 4, p. 246, for information about writing titles.

Final Draft Checklist

	YES	NO
▸ Did I include a thesis statement that contains a clear topic and controlling idea?	❑	❑
▸ Is this clearly a comparison essay? A contrast essay? An essay that discusses both comparison and contrast?	❑	❑
▸ Did I use a quotation to begin the essay? Why or why not?	❑	❑
▸ Did I use comparison-contrast essay transition expressions correctly?	❑	❑
▸ When I have multiple, equivalent items in a sentence, are they parallel?	❑	❑
▸ Did I use any comparative structures, superlative structures, or structures with *as . . . as* or *the same as?* If so, did I form them all correctly?	❑	❑
▸ Does each of my body paragraphs have a clear topic sentence?	❑	❑
▸ Does each body paragraph contain one subtopic?	❑	❑
▸ Does my concluding paragraph successfully signal the end of my essay? That is, does my concluding paragraph sound like a "final" paragraph?	❑	❑
▸ Does my entire essay have unity and coherence?	❑	❑

Additional Writing Assignments from the Academic Disciplines

Beginning with the Prewriting activity on p. 108, use the writing process and write another essay. Choose a topic from the following list.

SUBJECT	*WRITING TASK*
Business	Given today's economic situation, companies are seeking to maximize benefits from their expenses. In terms of advertising budgets, does it make more sense for a company to spend more money on Internet ads or traditional print ads?
Science	Compare/contrast two animals that are similar, for example, crocodiles and alligators.

alligator

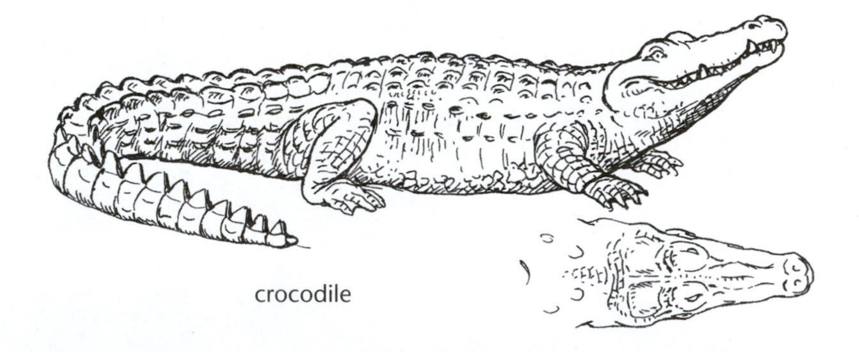

crocodile

History	Compare/contrast the lives of two important historical figures. Is one more important than the other? Why?
Linguistics	Compare/contrast two languages.
Travel	Compare/contrast two popular tourist destinations.

UNIT 5

Blueprints for

CAUSE/EFFECT ESSAYS

PART A

Blueprints for Cause/Effect Essays

Objectives	**In Part A, you will:**
Analysis:	learn about methods of organization in cause/effect essays
Unity and Coherence:	
Unity:	learn to focus on the relationship between causes and effects
Coherence: Transition Expressions:	learn to use *because/as/since* + s + v; *therefore; consequently; thus; as a result* + s + v/*as a result of*
Grammar Focus:	do a verb tense review
Sentence Check:	study fragments, run-ons, and comma splices
Practice:	practice organizing causes and effects

What Is a Cause/Effect Essay?

In cause/effect essays, writers focus on what causes something (why it happens) and what the effects are (the consequences or results). For example, you might write an essay about what causes unemployment and its consequences, or about the causes of hurricanes and their consequences.

Methods of Organization

You can organize a cause/effect essay according to the information that you want to present. You can focus on 1) only the causes of something leading to one effect, 2) only the effects resulting from one cause, 3) more than one cause leading to more than one effect, or 4) a chain reaction of cause leading to effect leading to cause leading to effect. The charts below show the many options you can use when you organize a cause/effect essay.

Method 1: Causes leading to only one effect

Example thesis:

The main causes of unemployment in the United States are downturns in the economy, lack of vocational or professional skills, and personal choice to be unemployed.

Cause 1 Cause 2 Cause 3

Method 2: Effects resulting from only one cause

Example thesis:

Unemployment can have terrible effects on individuals, including financial, psychological, and social difficulties.

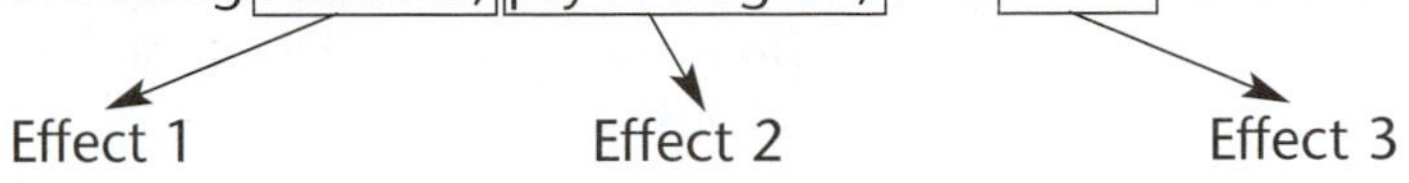

Effect 1 Effect 2 Effect 3

Method 3: Many causes having many effects

Example thesis:

The numerous factors that lead to unemployment can have disastrous effects on individuals.

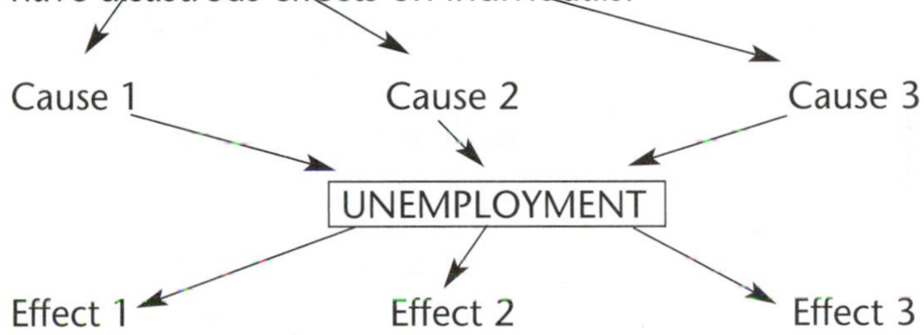

Effect 1 Effect 2 Effect 3

Method 4: A chain of causes leading to effect leading to cause leading to effect

Example thesis:

The loss of a job can sometimes lead to extreme actions such as suicide.

Cause → Effect . . . Cause → Effect... Cause → Effect

In this example, you would trace the causes and effects that could lead from unemployment to suicide.

NOTE: Later in this unit, you will be asked to choose one of the four methods to organize your cause/effect essay.

EXERCISE

Recognizing Methods of Organization

Each item provides information about planning a cause/effect essay. Read the information and circle the correct method of organization. Refer to the methods of organization above for help.

1. *Thesis Statement:* Young people join the military for many reasons.

   Body paragraph 1: One major reason is to get away from home.

   Body paragraph 2: Depending on the political climate, many young people join in order to serve their country.

Body paragraph 3: Because of the excellent educational support that the military offers, some people join to get university scholarships.

Method 1 **Method 2** **Method 3** **Method 4**

2. *Thesis Statement:* By winning the lottery, Dr. Kovacs became an influential politician.

   Body paragraph 1: Dr. Kovacs won the lottery and was featured on television.

   Body paragraph 2: Interviewers asked her questions ranging from her personal life to her political beliefs.

   Body paragraph 3: Television viewers saw the interviews and liked the message Dr. Kovacs was giving.

   Body paragraph 4: Because they liked the message, many people contacted Dr. Kovacs and suggested she run for office.

   Body paragraph 5: Dr. Kovacs took their suggestion, ran for office, and won a seat on her local city council.

   Method 1 **Method 2** **Method 3** **Method 4**

3. *Thesis Statement:* Daily reading has excellent benefits.

   Body Paragraph 1: People who read daily increase their vocabulary.

   Body Paragraph 2: Daily reading also causes an increased reading speed.

   Body Paragraph 3: Depending on the information that is read, people who read daily increase their general and specific knowledge.

   Method 1 **Method 2** **Method 3** **Method 4**

4. *Thesis Statement:* By practicing yoga, people can improve their physical, mental, and emotional well-being.

   Body Paragraph 1: Yoga can improve physical strength.

   Body Paragraph 2: To improve mental awareness, yoga exercises are very effective.

   Body Paragraph 3: People who practice yoga tend to experience emotional well-being.

   Method 1 **Method 2** **Method 3** **Method 4**

Unity in Cause/Effect Essays

A cause/effect essay should focus on one topic and explain causes and effects that are relevant to that topic. In other words, the focus should be sharp. To achieve unity, your readers need to be able to see clearly the relationship between causes and effects that you are presenting. (See Unit 1, pages 4–5 and 21–22 for more about unity in essays.)

EXERCISE 2

Focusing Causes and Effects

Read each thesis statement and the three statements that follow, which are either causes or effects. One of these cause or effect statements does not relate to the thesis. Work with a partner and circle the letter of the sentence that does not lend unity to the information.

1. THESIS: Learning a foreign language can have many positive benefits.

   a. A person can communicate with a wide variety of people.

   b. Learning a foreign language can also enhance one's understanding of another culture.

   c. Some languages are much more difficult to learn than others.

2. THESIS: Three main factors are connected with the onset of high cholesterol.

   a. High cholesterol is a dangerous affliction that can cause heart attacks.

   b. Some healthy people get high cholesterol through heredity when parents pass it down to children.

   c. High cholesterol can be attributed to unhealthy eating habits.

   d. Lack of exercise can also lead to a rise in cholesterol levels.

3. THESIS: Because of the sudden hurricane, the villagers are now migrating west.

   a. The hurricane caused massive destruction to homes and other buildings.

   b. Because the buildings were uninhabitable, the townspeople slept outdoors.

   c. These outdoor living conditions were very poor.

   d. The villagers applied for local, state, and federal aid.

   e. Aid was refused, so the villagers moved to other regions of the country.

Coherence in Cause/Effect Essays

In cause/effect essays, transition expressions help create coherence. (To review general information about coherence in essays, see Unit 1, pages 5–8.)

Transition Expressions

Transition Expressions: *because/as/since* + s + v; *therefore; consequently; thus; as a result* + s + v/*as a result of*

because/as/since **+ subject + verb**

Function: to give the cause of or reason for something

Use: *Because, as,* and *since* are subordinating conjunctions. Because these conjunctions introduce a dependent clause, they are followed by a subject and a verb. Note that these clauses CANNOT stand alone as independent sentences.

Examples: Because Rita was tired, she came home early from work. OR
Rita came home early from work because she was tired.

As the weather was too unpredictable, we were unable to make plans for the picnic. OR
We were unable to make plans for the picnic as the weather was too unpredictable.

Since the tuition for Yale University was too high, John decided to study at the City University of New York. OR
John decided to study at the City University of New York since the tuition for Yale University was too high.

Punctuation note: When the dependent clause beginning with *because, as,* or *since* comes at the beginning of the sentence, put a comma after it.

therefore/ consequently/ thus **+ subject + verb**

Function: to show the result of something

Use: *Therefore, consequently,* and *thus* are conjunctive adverbs. They connect the previous information (cause) to the following information (effect.) Because these adverbs introduce sentences (independent clauses), they are followed by a subject and a verb.

Examples: Rita was tired. Therefore, she came home early from work.

The weather was unpredictable. Consequently, we were unable to make plans for the picnic.

The tuition for Yale University was too high; thus, John decided to study at the City University of New York.

(continued)

(continued)

Punctuation note: When these transition words begin a new sentence, put a comma after the word. If the transition word connects one sentence to another, put a semicolon before the word and a comma after it.

as a result + s + v/as a result of

Function: to signal the effect of something

Use: *As a result* and *as a result of* are commonly used at the beginning of a sentence to show the effects or results of a previous action. *As a result* introduces an independent clause and is followed by a subject and a verb. *As a result of* is followed by a noun.

Examples: Rita was extremely tired. As a result, she went home from work early.

As a result of her fatigue, Rita went home from work early.

Punctuation note: *As a result* is followed by a comma.

Blueprint Cause/Effect Essays

In this section, you will read and analyze two sample cause/effect essays. These essays can act as blueprints when you write your own cause/effect essay in Part B.

Blueprint Cause/Effect Essay 1: Marketing Health and Fitness

PREREADING DISCUSSION QUESTIONS

1. *Have you ever been on a diet? If so, did it work well for you? Why or why not?*
2. *Do you think there is a "perfect" body type? Why or why not? Which body type do you think most people would call "perfect?"*

EXERCISE 3

Reading and Answering Questions

Read the cause/effect essay. Then answer the questions that follow.

Marketing Health and Fitness

boom: increase; burst of growth

infiltrate: permeate; filter into

bombard: attack; continuously show

1 Americans spend between $30 and $60 billion a year on dieting. This amount is more than the gross national product for Morocco! Such spending has not always been the case. Only recently has the marketing **boom** on health, fitness, and dieting **infiltrated** American televisions, radios, and magazines. The message is clear: getting healthy through diet and exercise is a necessary part of life. As Americans continue to be **bombarded** with these health-conscious images, it is evident that the images have altered Americans' ideas about health. The current advertising trends in weight loss and fitness have had both positive and negative effects.

2 Perhaps the most positive effect of dieting and weight loss advertising is an increase in education. For many years Americans ate heavy foods cooked only in butter or lard. In addition, exercise was considered appropriate only for men. These trends changed as television and radio began promoting a healthier lifestyle that includes private gyms, low calorie foods, and aerobics tapes, among other things. As a result of this advertisement, Americans began to understand that diet, exercise, and other preventive measures made them healthier. They are now aware that heart disease and other illnesses can be controlled with proper diet and exercise. Since the media's attention to this phenomenon, Americans are certainly healthier than they were in the recent past.

barrage: blast

emulate: imitate; copy

3 Although the current trends in weight loss have made Americans more conscious of their health, they have also led to increased public pressure. This is true for teenagers, especially girls. Adolescents cannot escape the constant **barrage** of ads on television and radio and in magazines and newspapers. While some teenagers take this new-found knowledge and begin eating more appropriate foods and exercising regularly, others become obsessed with weight loss. As a result, these young people can develop eating disorders such as *bulimia* and *anorexia nervosa* to try to **emulate** the physiques of models and health promoters. In these cases, the focus on fit and healthy bodies has a negative effect.

4 The financial effects of health industry ads cannot be avoided. Americans spend billions of dollars each year trying to get fit. Consumers will spend whatever they have to in order to get the latest gym equipment, fat-free food, or diet supplement pill. Because all these marketing strategies promote healthy living, many people are spending excessive amounts of money on such products. Consequently, the diet industry continues to promote newer and 'better' products.

5 Marketing strategies have changed public opinion in many areas, and the idea that everyone should have a perfect body is a major example

(continued)

(continued)

of this. Knowledge is power, and Americans should learn as much as they can about health and fitness. Then they should use that knowledge in healthful ways.

POSTREADING QUESTIONS

1. *Read the hook (first sentence) of the essay. This is called a* ***dramatic statement,*** *an interesting piece of information that engages the reader to continue with the essay. In your opinion, why is this sentence dramatic?* ______________________________

   ____

   ____

2. *Read the thesis statement. Is it direct or indirect?* ______________
3. *Refer to the methods of organization on pages 118–119. Which method does this essay use, 1, 2, 3, or 4?* ______________
4. *How many effects are discussed in this essay?* ______________
5. *Separate the effects into positive and negative.*

   Positive effect(s): ______________________________

   ____

   Negative effect(s): ______________________________

   ____

6. *In the conclusion paragraph, what is the author's opinion about the marketing of health products?* ______________________________

   ____

   ____

Blueprint Cause/Effect Essay 2: Why Plastic Surgery?

PREREADING DISCUSSION QUESTIONS

1. *Do you know someone who has had plastic surgery? What kind of surgery did they have? Was it successful? Explain.*
2. *Would you ever consider having it done? Why or why not?*

EXERCISE 4

Reading and Answering Questions

Read the cause/effect essay. Fill in the blanks with transition expressions from the list below. Use one of the words twice. Then answer the post-reading questions.

consequently   As a result of these operations   because   therefore

Why Plastic Surgery?

1 It seems impossible to imagine that the first cosmetic surgery was performed in antiquity, but it is true. By 3400 BC, Egyptians had already performed operations to reshape body tissues. Granted, the procedure of plastic surgery has undergone many changes and advancements since then, but one thing is clear. In today's society, people still want to alter their appearance for one reason or another. Just why are people **tempted** to undergo plastic surgery? The main reasons are for personal satisfaction, social acceptance, and professional advancement.

tempted: fascinated

2 The majority of people who **undergo aesthetic** plastic surgery say that they are doing it ____________________ they want to feel better about themselves. These are people who, when they look in the mirror, see nothing but a huge nose or elephant ears. They don't necessarily care about what others think; ____________________, they believe that they are going to feel better about themselves after having plastic surgery. These operations can range from small **nips and tucks** to complete makeovers. The bottom line is that the patients have an internal desire to please themselves.

undergo: experience

aesthetic: pleasing to the eye; beautiful

nips and tucks: minor plastic surgery procedures such as wrinkle reductions

(continued)

conform: comply with; obey

augmentation: increase

(continued)

3 Another cause for wanting plastic surgery is to **conform** to social norms. For example, some women dream of appearing "model-like." ____________________, they may have fat injected into their lips. Men are more likely to have their breasts reduced because they feel that their torsos are "unnatural" if their breasts are too meaty. These types of operations are often reflections of the current trends in body types.

4 Perhaps the most bizarre reason for plastic surgery is for professional development. While this phenomenon is not widely discussed, there are a number of people who alter their physical appearances in order to be more successful actors, dancers, or models. It is not uncommon to hear about starlets who have breast **augmentations** or, less frequently, breast reductions performed. ____________________, these people can be more "marketable."

5 A practice that has been around for almost three thousand years will certainly not disappear any time soon. In fact, the number of plastic surgery operations performed is growing steadily. However, before turning to the knife to alter physical appearance, it is important to ask the simple question, "Why?"

POSTREADING DISCUSSION QUESTIONS

1. *What is the thesis statement of this essay? Write it here.*

   ____

2. *The introductory paragraph contains a dramatic statement as a hook. In your opinion, why is the beginning of the essay dramatic?*

   ____

3. *The controlling idea of a topic sentence is the idea that will be discussed in the paragraph. Write each of the controlling ideas discussed in the essay.*

   Paragraph 2: ______________________________

   Paragraph 3: ______________________________

   Paragraph 4: ______________________________

4. *Read the conclusion. Is there any information from the conclusion that can be connected to the hook, or dramatic statements, of the essay? If yes, what is it?* ______________________________

____

Grammar Focus and Sentence Check

Grammar Focus: Verb Tense Review

The three main verb tenses are the present, the past, and the future. Within these tenses are several different options.

Present tense

1. The simple present is used for things that are generally known to be true.

   Examples: Water *boils* at 212 degrees Fahrenheit.

   The planets *rotate* around the sun.

   The simple present can also be used for events that are true now.

   Examples: Harold *works* at IBM.

   My mother and father *are* on vacation.

2. The present progressive (or present continuous) takes the form *(am/is/are)* + ***MAIN VERB*** + *ing*. It is used to describe what is happening at this moment.

   Examples: Brittany and Lisa *are watching* TV.

   The dogs *are barking* and *waking* up all the neighbors.

3. The present continuous can also describe an action that will occur in the immediate future. In this usage, the actual time is usually stated directly (see underlined parts of the sentence).

   Examples: I *am going* to the mall <u>this afternoon.</u>

   The members of the European Community *are meeting* in the Hague <u>in a few weeks.</u>

Present perfect tense

The present perfect takes the form *have/has* + past participle of the main verb. Because of its many uses, the present perfect can fall into three general categories: 1) indefinite past, 2) repeated past action, and 3) continuation of an action from the past to now.

Examples:

1. indefinite past tense

   Brianna *has seen* that movie. (She saw that movie at some unspecified time in the past.)

2. repeated past action, which may or may not happen again

   The Brazilian National Soccer Team *has won* the World Cup at least four times. (The action was repeated in the past.)

3. continuation of an action from the past to now

   The French language students *have studied* together since January. (They began to study in the past and continue in the present. This form is usually expressed with *since* and *for.* Common verbs for this usage are *live, study, work,* and *wear.*)

Past tense

1. The past tense describes actions that happened in the past. The simple past refers to an action that is finished. It began and ended in the past.

   Examples: John F. Kennedy *died* in 1963.

   I *finished* the book last night.

2. The past tense can also take the progressive form of *was/were* + ***MAIN** VERB* + *ing*

   This tense is commonly used for an action that was happening at a specific time in the past.

   Example: Last night at 7:30 I *was eating* dinner with my family.

   The past progressive can also explain an action that was interrupted by something (usually another action). The interruption often includes the word *when.*

   Example: We *were studying* in the library *when* the fire alarm went off.

   When you refer to two things that occurred at the same time, use *while* with the first action and put both verbs in the past progressive.

   Example: While the instructor *was grading* the essays, the students *were taking* a grammar test.

Future tense

Form the simple future most often by using the modal verb *will* + *MAIN VERB.*

Example: The congressional leaders *will meet* in the near future to discuss the proposed bill.

Another way of forming the simple future tense is to use *be going to* + *MAIN VERB.*

Example: The congressional leaders *are going to meet* in the near future to discuss the proposed bill.

EXERCISE

IDENTIFYING VERB TENSES IN ESSAYS

Reread Blueprints Essay 1 on pp. 124–125. Then answer the questions.

1. Find the sentences in paragraph 1 that use the present perfect tense. Underline them.
2. In paragraph 2, which two verb tenses are used?

   ____

Reread Blueprints Essay 2 on pp. 126–127. Then answer the questions.

3. Find the sentence in paragraph 1 that uses the past perfect. Underline it.
4. In paragraph 2, find the sentence that uses the future tense. Write it here. ______________________________

EXERCISE

WORKING WITH VERB TENSES

Read the following sentences. In the blanks, write the correct form of the verb that is shown in parentheses ( ).

1. Belinda and her brother (work) ______________ in the library right now, but they (be) ______________ home later this evening.
2. The people who take the subway usually (commute) ______________ to the city but (live) ______________ in the suburbs.
3. What time do your parents usually (wake up) ______________ in the mornings?
4. Don't talk to Gretchen right now. She (watch) ______________ her favorite program on TV.

5 How many times (Bob see) ________________ that movie?

6. Yesterday while the students (talk) ________________ to the professor, she (look) ________________ in the textbook.

EXERCISE 7

Working with Verb Tenses and Transition Expressions

Read the following sentences. In the blanks, write the correct form of the verb that is shown in parentheses ( ). Then rewrite each sentence to include one of the transition expressions listed. The first one is done for you.

because as a result of therefore since consequently

1. We (want) wanted to go to the beach yesterday, but it (be) was too cloudy.

   Because it was too cloudy, we didn't go to the beach yesterday.

2. Dr. Goldstein's biology class (study) ________________ for the final exam for the past two weeks. The majority of the students did very well.

   ____

   ____

3. My dog (chew) ________________ my favorite shoes when I got home from work. I (be) ________________ so angry at her.

   ____

   ____

4. This afternoon Bill and Jim decided that the airline tickets to Pheonix (be) ________________ too expensive. They (decide) ________________ to take a bus instead.

   ____

   ____

Sentence Check: Fragments, Run-ons, and Comma Splices

Three of the most common errors in English sentences are **fragments, run-ons,** and **comma splices.** It is important to learn to recognize and correct these errors.

Fragments

A fragment is an incomplete sentence. It is missing a crucial element, usually either the subject or the verb, and sometimes a whole clause. To correct a fragment, add the missing part.

Examples:

Fragment	Is a very nice day. (missing a subject)
Correction	**It** is a very nice day.
Fragment	My birthday Tuesday. (missing a verb)
Correction	My birthday **is** Tuesday.
Fragment	Because he wanted to lose weight. (missing an independent clause)
Correction	**Mario joined a health club** because he wanted to lose weight.

Run-on Sentences

A run-on sentence contains two complete thoughts (two sentences) that are connected without any form of punctuation. To correct a run-on sentence, add punctuation between the two sentences or create two separate sentences.

Examples:

Run-on	Society has an obligation to help those in need this includes government support and privately funded donations.
Correction	Society has an obligation to help those in need**;** this includes government support and privately funded donations.
Correction	Society has an obligation to help those in need. **This** includes government support and privately funded donations.

Comma Splices

A comma splice is two sentences connected only by a comma. There are a few ways to correct a comma splice.

1. Put a semicolon (;) between the two sentences instead of a comma.

Example:

Comma splice	The effects of long-term exposure to the sun are not pleasant, people can suffer from skin cancer as well as from other epidermal illnesses.

Correction The effects of long-term exposure to the sun are not pleasant; people can suffer from skin cancer as well as from other epidermal illnesses.

2. Add a conjunction after the comma.

Example:

Correction The effects of long-term exposure to the sun are not pleasant, **for** people can suffer from skin cancer as well as other epidermal illnesses

3. Use a period to create two separate sentences.

Example:

Correction The effects of long-term exposure to the sun are not pleasant**. People** can suffer from skin cancer as well as other epidermal illnesses

EXERCISE

Identifying Fragments, Run-ons, and Comma Splices

Read the following sentences. Identify them as either fragments (FRAG), run-ons (RO), comma splices (CS), or correct (C)

_______ 1. In the freshman English class, the first semester focuses on writing the second semester focuses more on literature.

_______ 2. Because we were all extremely prepared for the final exam.

_______ 3. The monastery's doors have been closed to the public for one hundred years.

_______ 4. Carol is not in law school, she's in medical school.

_______ 5. Since it was the first day of summer.

_______ 6. The possibilities are endless, but the timing must be correct.

EXERCISE

Correcting Fragments, Run-ons, and Comma Splices

Reread the sentences in Exercise 8. Correct the fragments, run-ons, and comma splices. There may be more that one way to correct the errors.

EXERCISE 10

Editing Practice: Grammar Focus and Sentence Check Application

Read this paragraph carefully. Find and correct the eight errors in verb tense, fragments, run-ons, or comma splices. The first one is done for you.

Italians are becoming more and more angry at the sights they see on television, in almost every type of programming, models known as "soubrettes" or "letterine" were common sights. What do these women do? The answer, which upsets the majority of Italians, is . . . nothing. They stand on stage, wear extremely skimpy outfits, and pose for the camera. Appear on game shows, variety shows, sports shows, and even documentaries. While they are beautiful and, many argue, very nice to look at. They are having a negative effect on the youth of Italy. Adolescent girls are being encouraged to look good and nothing else. They didn't need entertainment skills such as singing, dancing, or interviewing all that is required to become a soubrette is a hard body, full lips, and the ability to smile for the camera. With European unity in full swing. Italian mass media hopes to set the standard of quality television, however, with this type of programming, Italians will only succeed in becoming the laughing stocks of a united Europe.

PART B

The Writing Process: Practice Writing a Cause/Effect Essay

Objectives	In Part B, you will:
Prewriting:	practice using a spoke diagram to get ideas for your cause/effect essay
Planning:	use a chart to organize and sequence ideas
Partner Feedback:	review classmates' charts and analyze feedback
First Draft:	write a cause/effect essay
	use a dramatic statement as an introductory technique
Partner Feedback:	review classmates' essays and analyze feedback
Final Draft:	use feedback to write a final draft of your cause/effect essay

The Writing Process: Writing Assignment

IMPORTANT NOTE:

If an instructor in another class gives you an assignment that requires you to write a cause/effect essay, how do you know if you should write a cause-only essay, an effects-only essay, or an essay about both causes and effects? One way is to ask your instructor to put the assignment in question form, for example, "What were the reasons for the creation of the United Nations?" Even though the words *cause* and *effect* do not appear in the question, the topic is an effect (the creation of the United Nations) and you need to explain what the causes, or reasons, were.

Your assignment is to write an essay about the causes and effects of technological advances on a specific career or field of study. After you complete the Prewriting and Planning sections, you will decide whether your essay will follow method 1 (causes of technological advances), method 2 (effects of technological advances), or method 3 (causes and effects of technological advances). See pp. 118–119 to review these organizational methods. Then follow the steps in the writing process in this section.

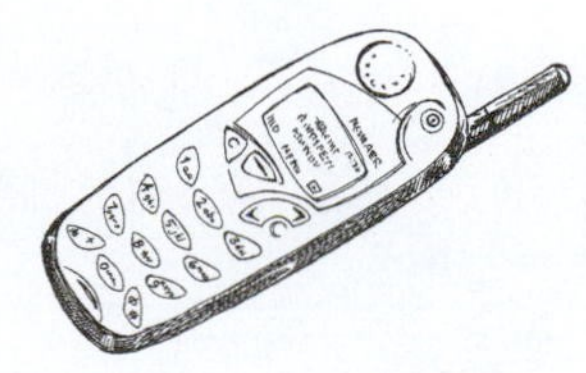

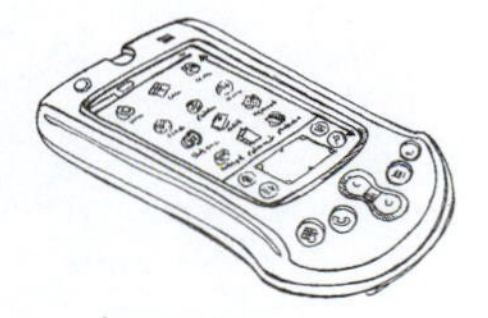

Prewriting: Using a Spoke Diagram

A spoke diagram is a useful way of generating ideas for a cause/effect essay. In a spoke diagram, you put a topic in a central box or circle and draw arrows out from it, like the spokes on a wheel. Each arrow points to an idea that relates to the topic. The following questions may help you think of causes and effects that are related to your topic:

- How is this career or field of study different now from what it was 20 or 30 years ago?
- In what specific ways has this career or field of study changed?
- Why has it changed?
- What is different because of modern technology?

Here is a sample of a spoke diagram on the subject of illegal drugs in the Olympic Games. Notice that the writer includes ideas for both the causes of illegal drug use and the effects of it. The writer will not use all the ideas in the final essay.

Topic: The causes and/or effects of illegal drugs in the Olympic Games

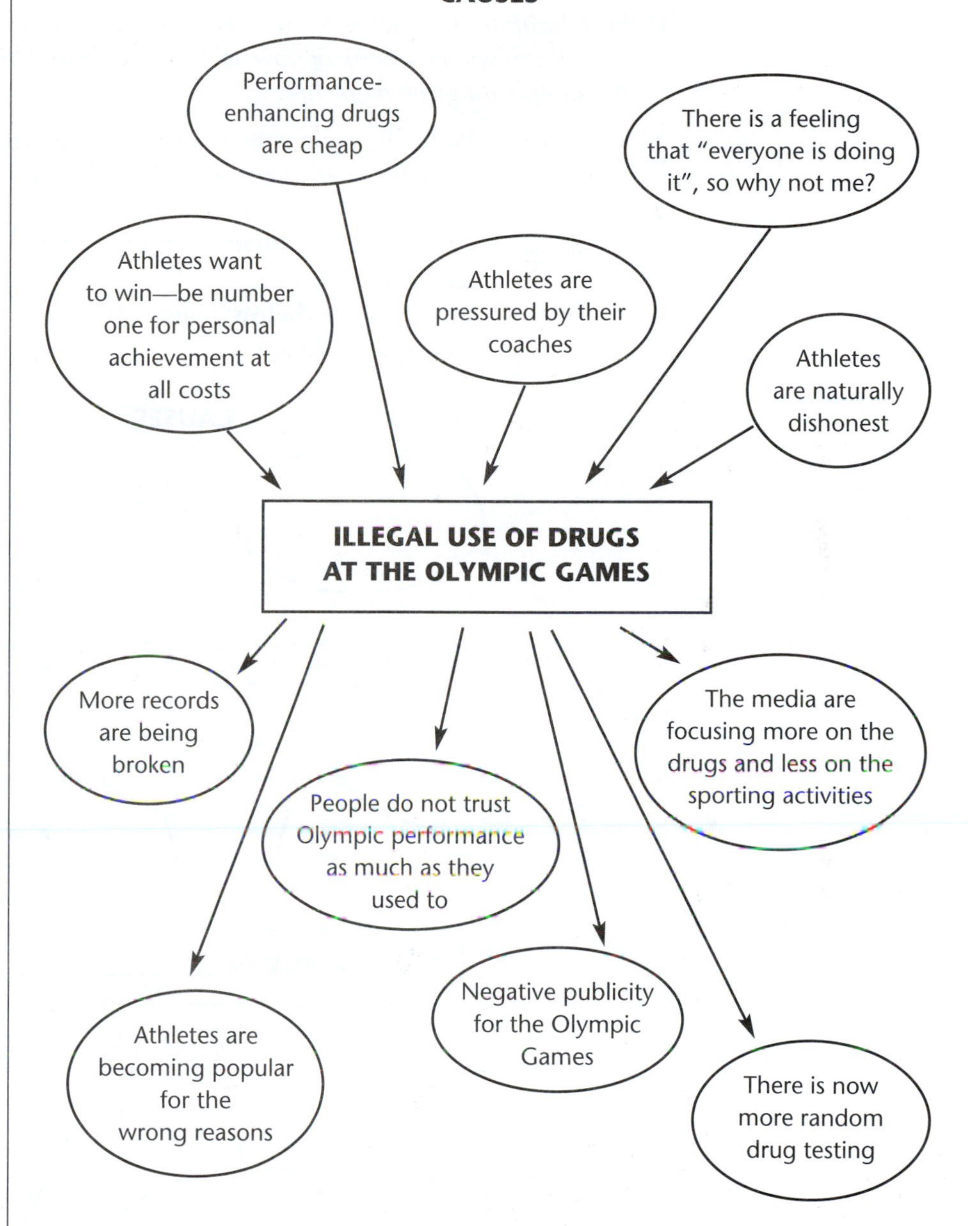

EXERCISE 11

Creating a Spoke Diagram

Use the spoke diagram to record ideas for writing your cause/effect essay. The following steps will help you fill in the diagram. Remember that you will be eliminating some of these ideas in the planning stage, so just write everything you can think of now. If you need help with this diagram, look at the sample diagram on p. 137.

STEP 1: Write the main subject of your essay (modern technology and a specific career or field of study) in the box in the center of the page.

STEP 2: In the circles **above** your topic, write the CAUSES for the technology change.

STEP 3: In the circles **below** your topic, write the EFFECTS of this technology change.

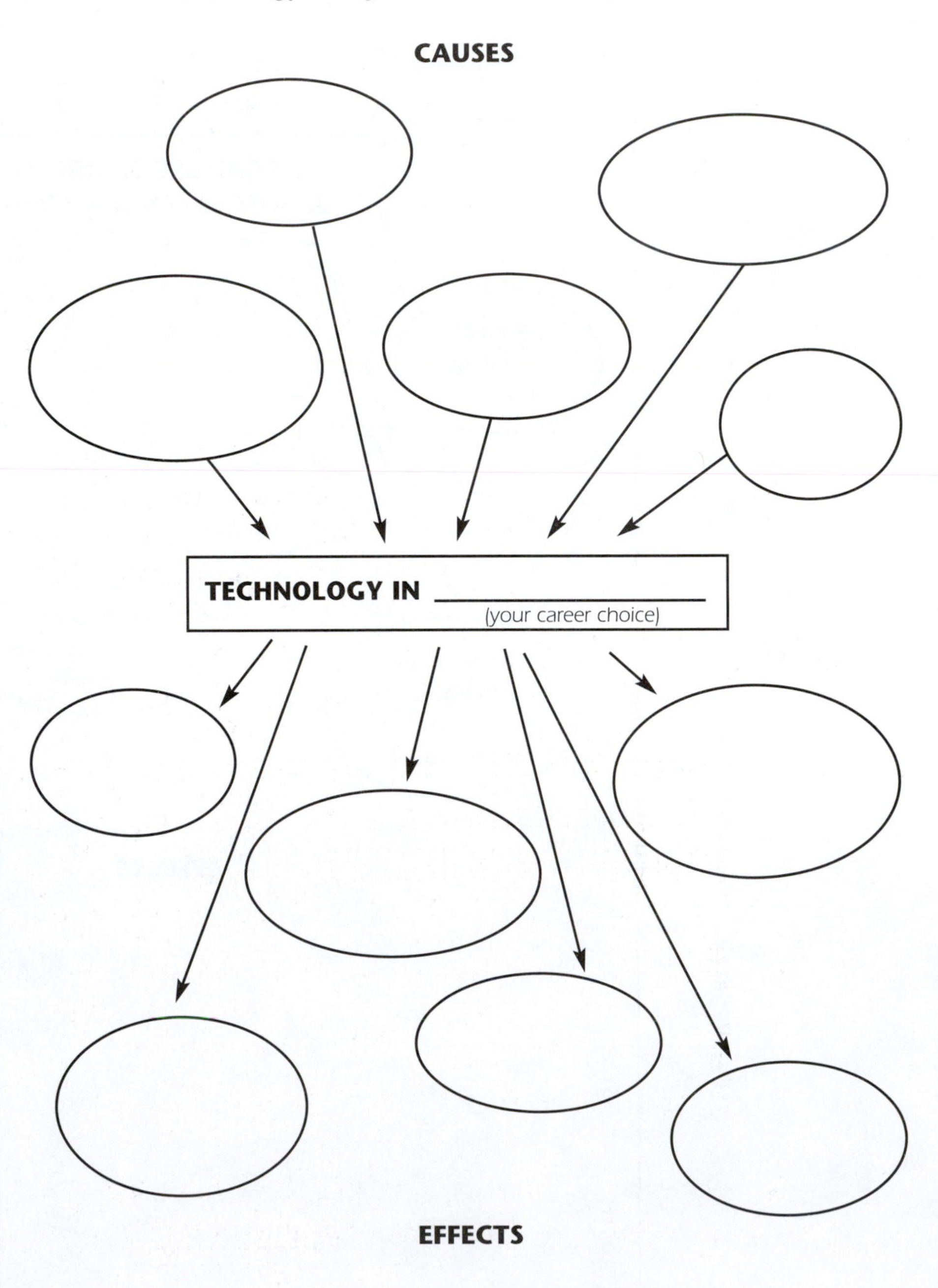

Planning: Creating a Cause/Effect Chart

After the writer filled in her spoke diagram, she decided to plan the essay by organizing her information using a cause/effect chart. During this process, she discarded some of her original ideas and added some supporting details. Her chart ended up looking like this.

ILLEGAL DRUG USE IN THE OLYMPIC GAMES

CAUSES	EFFECTS
1. Athletes want to win.	1. More records are being broken.
Strong/unhealthy spirit of competition.	Give examples, names, dates
Want to be famous world-wide.	
2. Athletes are pressured by others.	2. There is more testing nowadays.
Ex: family, coaches, friends	Special organizations that test
Pressure from media	Random test results available
3. Athletes see others doing it.	3. People trust Olympic performance less.
Doesn't seem "bad"	Public disbelieving new records
Makes them equal to other athletes	Ex: Irish swimmer in 2000 games

In her chart, the writer was able to list supporting information for three causes and three effects of illegal drug use by athletes. As a result, she believes she has enough material to write an essay that will focus on both causes and effects. So she chooses Method 3 (causes and effects) as her essay's organizational method.

EXERCISE 12

FILLING IN A CAUSE/EFFECT CHART

Fill in the blank chart with causes and effects from your spoke diagram in Exercise 11. Then write as many supporting details as you can think of for each cause and each effect. When you are finished, follow the directions below the chart.

TECHNOLOGY AND ____________________

CAUSES	EFFECTS
1.	1.
2.	2.
3.	3.
4.	4.
5.	5.

Now review your chart. Did you list more causes than effects? Do your ideas seem stronger for effects than for causes? Are your lists evenly distributed? Depending on the answers to these questions, you can now choose which method of organization you will use: 1 (causes only), 2 (effects only), or 3 (causes and effects).

Cross out any ideas that you do not want to use. The remaining information in your chart will be the basis of your essay.

Partner Feedback Form 1

Exchange your cause/effect chart with another student. Read your partner's chart and answer the questions on Partner Feedback Form 1: Unit 5, p. 235, in Appendix 3. Discuss your partner's reactions to your chart. Make notes about any parts you need to change before you write your paper. For more information about giving partner feedback, see Appendix 2, p. 218, Guidelines for Partner Feedback.

First Draft

Now you are ready to write the first draft of your essay. Before you begin, review your cause/effect chart and any comments from your partner, especially the thesis statement suggestion.

EXERCISE 13

Writing the Introduction

Write an introduction for your topic, using your chart and the feedback you received from your partner. Use a dramatic statement as explained on p. 16, Unit 1 to begin your essay. Both "Marketing Health and Fitness" on pp. 124–125 and "Why Plastic Surgery?" on pp. 126–127 use this introduction technique. You can use them as models if you want. End your introduction with a well-constructed thesis statement. When you finish, use the checklist to review your work.

IMPORTANT NOTE:

A dramatic statement can be any piece of interesting information about your topic. It can be a surprising statistic or statement, a brief story, or any other piece of interesting information that is related to your thesis statement.

- Try to make your dramatic statement surprising—something that your writer does not know about.
- Your dramatic statement should be followed by further background information that leads smoothly to the thesis statement.

Introduction Checklist

	YES	NO
▸ Did I use an effective dramatic statement—a surprising fact or interesting story to introduce my topic?	❑	❑
▸ Does my introduction flow logically from the hook of the dramatic statement to the thesis?	❑	❑
▸ Does my thesis statement provide a clear indication of the Method of Organization I will use in the essay (1, 2, 3, or 4)?	❑	❑
▸ Is the purpose of my essay clear?	❑	❑

What is it? ______________________

EXERCISE 14

Writing Body Paragraphs

Look again at your chart for your cause/effect essay. Then complete the body paragraphs. When you finish, use the checklist to review your work.

Body Paragraph Checklist

	YES	NO
▸ Does each body paragraph in my essay treat only one main idea?	❑	❑
▸ Does each contain a topic sentence with a clear controlling idea?	❑	❑
▸ Does each paragraph end with a logical concluding sentence?	❑	❑
▸ Do my body paragraphs all relate to and support the thesis statement of the essay? In other words, do they each discuss a cause and/or effect mentioned in my thesis statement?	❑	❑
▸ Are the relationships between causes and effects clear to the reader?	❑	❑
▸ Are all the supporting sentences in my body paragraphs relevant to the topic? That is, do they have unity?	❑	❑

EXERCISE 15

Writing a Conclusion

*Review again your **cause/effect chart,** partner feedback form, introduction, and body. Write a conclusion for your essay. When you finish, use the checklist to review your work.*

Conclusion Checklist

	YES	NO
▸ Does my conclusion successfully signal the end of my essay?	❑	❑
▸ Does my conclusion add coherence to the essay by:		
a. restating the essay thesis?	❑	❑
b. summarizing or restating the essay subtopics?	❑	❑
▸ Does my conclusion:		
a. leave the reader with my final thoughts?	❑	❑
b. offer a suggestion, an opinion, or a prediction about the topic of the essay?	❑	❑

Partner Feedback Form 2

Exchange essays with another student. Read your partner's essay and answer the questions on Partner Feedback Form 2: Unit 5, p. 237, in Appendix 3. Discuss your partner's reactions to your essay. Make notes about any parts you need to change before your write your second draft. For more information about giving partner feedback, see Appendix 2, p. 218, Guidelines for Partner Feedback.

Final Draft

Carefully revise your essay using all the feedback you have received: partner feedback review of your chart and essay, instructor comments, and any evaluation you have done yourself. Use the checklist to do a final check of your essay. In addition, try reading your essay aloud. This can help you find awkward-sounding sentences and errors in punctuation. When you have finished, add a title to your essay and neatly type your final draft. See Appendix 4, p. 246, for information about writing titles.

Final Draft Checklist

	YES	NO
▸ Did I use a dramatic statement to introduce the essay?	❑	❑
▸ Will my dramatic statement hook my audience? Why or why not? ______________________	❑	❑
▸ Did I include a thesis statement that contains a clear topic and controlling idea?	❑	❑
▸ Is my method of organization obvious?	❑	❑
▸ Did I use transition expressions correctly?	❑	❑
▸ Did I use verb tense correctly?	❑	❑
▸ Are my sentences free of run-ons, fragments, and comma splices?	❑	❑
▸ Does each of my body paragraphs have a clear topic sentence?	❑	❑
▸ Does each body paragraph contain one subtopic?	❑	❑
▸ Does my concluding paragraph successfully signal the end of my essay? That is, does my concluding paragraph sound like a "final" paragraph?	❑	❑
▸ Does my entire essay have unity and coherence?	❑	❑

Additional Writing Assignments from the Academic Disciplines

Beginning with the Prewriting activity on p. 136, use the writing process to write another cause/effect essay. Choose a topic from the following list.

SUBJECT	*WRITING TASK*
Business	What are the effects of penny stocks on investors?
Science	What are the causes of a particular disease?
Technology	What are the effects on both high school students and admissions offices of submitting college applications on the Internet?
Geology	What are the causes and/or effects of earthquakes?
Current Issues	What are the causes and/or effects of homelessness?

UNIT 6

Blueprints for REACTION ESSAYS

PART A

Blueprints for Reaction Essays

Objectives	**In Part A, you will:**
Analysis:	identify and analyze a reaction essay
Unity and Coherence:	
Unity:	learn about background to unify a reaction essay
Coherence:	practice repeating key terms or phrases, using a pronoun to refer to a previous noun or noun phrase, and using synonyms
Grammar Focus:	study word forms
Sentence Check:	study sentence variety
Practice:	organize and write a reaction essay

What Is a Reaction Essay?

A very common type of writing task, one that appears in every academic discipline, is the **reaction essay.** In a reaction essay, the writer is usually given a prompt—a visual or written stimulus—to think about and respond to. A reaction essay focuses on the writer's feelings, opinions, and personal observations about the particular prompt.

IMPORTANT NOTE:

A prompt can be any number of things: a unit from a textbook, a piece of literature, a theory, a song, a picture, an article, a television program, a lecture, etc. Your instructor will often provide you with a prompt to generate the reaction essay.

EXERCISE 1

Practicing Reactions

Practice writing short reactions to the following stimuli. As you look at the pictures or read the item, answer these questions: How do you feel? What emotions are you experiencing? Explain why. Then compare your answers with a classmate's.

1. ______________________________

____

____

____

____

2. "To be or not to be; that is the question."—William Shakespeare

3.

4.

ANNOUNCEMENT:

Starting next semester, all first-year students will be required to do community service as part of their college education. Please contact the office for more information.

Dean of Undergraduate Studies

IMPORTANT NOTE:

You may want to use a combination of description, summary, and facts as background information in your introductory paragraph.

Unity in Reaction Essays

In order to create unity in a reaction essay, it is important to give the reader some background information about the prompt before you react to it. This background aids the reader in understanding what you are reacting to. It is important to maintain objective thought in the background information. The body of the essay will focus on your personal reaction, but you should begin with background information. (See Unit 1, pp. 4–5 and 21–22, for more about unity in essays.)

Background information varies based on the type of stimulus you are reacting to.

1. *Description:* If you are reacting to a *visual prompt,* the background information is usually a physical description of the item.
2. *Summary:* If you are reacting to a *written prompt,* you can give a summary of it in the introduction. Present the most important elements and follow the order of the original.
3. *Facts:* If you are reacting to a historical *event* or a *theory,* give factual information about it: specific dates, times, actions, and circumstances.

EXERCISE 2

Categorizing Background Information

Read the following reaction essay prompts. Working with a partner, decide if the background information should be a summary, *a* description, *or* factual information. *More than one answer is possible. The first one is done for you.*

1. the book *A Farewell to Arms* summary
2. the painting *Mona Lisa* ________________
3. the Battle of the Bulge in World War II ________________
4. the song *Give Peace a Chance* ________________
5. the movie *To Kill a Mockingbird* ________________
6. the lecture "Developing Countries and their Economic Needs"

   ____
7. a rejection letter from a university ________________

Coherence in Reaction Essays

In reaction essays, you create coherence with key terms, pronouns, and synonyms. (To review general information about coherence in essays, see Unit 1, pp. 4–8).

Coherence Techniques

1. Repeating Key Terms or Phrases. This helps readers stay focused on the subject you are discussing.

   Examples:

   The use of *symbolism* in Lisa's short story was fascinating. This *symbolism* was found throughout the story.

   The *Concorde* is the fastest passenger jet in the world. However, after a terrible crash in 2000, many people wondered if the *Concorde* was a safe airplane.

2. Using a pronoun to refer to a previous noun or noun phrase.

This method adds coherence by helping readers clearly follow the flow of information.

   Examples:

   Rhonda shocked everyone in her family. *She* decided to become a hot-air balloonist.

   The *system* of checks and balances is used to guarantee that none of the three branches of government has too much power. *It* promotes equity of power.

3. Using synonyms. Synonyms help maintain coherence by avoiding unnecessary repetition of information.

   Examples:

   The *Olympic Games* are played every four years in different countries. This *international competition* involves thousands of athletes from around the world.

   J.D. Salinger became an international success for his book *The Catcher in the Rye.* This novel touched millions of young people's lives.

EXERCISE 3

PRACTICING COHERENCE

Read the following paragraphs. Underline and identify the three coherence devices and write KT *(repetition of key term),* P *(pronoun), or* S *(synonym) above them.* ***The first two readings have the key words underlined to help you.***

1. Dr. Louis' lecture took place at 8 P.M. last night. His important lecture covered a wide variety of historical topics, including political warfare in Africa and its effects on the local population. This conflict has been going on for more than twenty years, and it will probably continue for the foreseeable future.

2. The TOEFL® is a trademarked exam created by Educational Testing Service. This exam evaluates student performance in the skills of listening comprehension, grammar and written expression, reading comprehension, and, more recently, essay writing. These skills are necessary in order to achieve academic success in university settings. The TOEFL® is widely used in the United States and Canada, and it is administered through testing centers around the world.

3. I wonder who the creator of the hourglass was. I wonder how this person changed people's lives by this invention. What did they use it for? Did they appreciate this hourglass or end up resenting it?

4. Although many people in Europe and Asia still smoke, this habit is becoming more and more taboo. Lawmakers are now prohibiting smoking in public areas. These countries are realizing the actual risk that cigarette smoke has to nonsmokers. A steep decline in public smoking areas will definitely improve people's health.

Blueprint Reaction Essays

In this section, you will read and analyze two sample reaction essays. These essays can act as blueprints when you write your own reaction essay in Part B.

Blueprint Reaction Essay 1: The Hourglass and Me

PREREADING DISCUSSION QUESTIONS

1. *What is the object pictured?*
2. *What is its purpose?*
3. *What do you feel when you look at this picture?*

EXERCISE 4

Reading and Answering Questions

Read the reaction essay. Then answer the questions that follow.

The Hourglass and Me

fine: very small

grains: small particles

static: unmoving; stagnant

persistently: in the manner of not stopping

resenting: feeling insulted; taking offense; disliking

crevice: gap; small opening; fissure

exotic: strikingly unfamiliar or unusual

1 Its shape is rather simple. It is rounded at the top and the bottom but pinched in the middle. Inside it are **fine grains** of sand. This is not a **static** object. The grains fall slowly but **persistently** from the upper portion to the lower portion. The hourglass, used to measure time, has a lot more meaning to me besides being a timepiece.

2 When I look at an hourglass, one of the primary images that comes to mind is history. Before the days of accurate timepieces, people had to use *something* that measured time. I wonder who the creator of the hourglass was. I wonder how the lives of people were changed by this invention. What did they use it for? Did they appreciate this hourglass or end up **resenting** it?

3 On a more personal level, the hourglass gives me a feeling of futility. Time is passing, and I can see it. It is right there in front of me. I cannot lie to myself and tell myself that I will do what I need to do tomorrow or the next day. I had better hurry up and do something with my life before the grains of sand have all fallen through the **crevice.** The picture is there, and it does not lie. I cannot escape time.

4 The reaction I feel from looking at an hourglass is also appreciation of simple beauty. The **exotic** curves of the glass flow so smoothly that I feel this hourglass is a living thing, not man-made. There really is something beautiful about the hourglass shape. It calls to me, and I end up feeling close to this innocent-looking device. It is clean and pure.

5 While the hourglass is not a classic piece of art, this small simple mechanism carries with it much power. The thoughts and emotions that come to my mind as I see it stimulate my sense of self. The power of the hourglass is inspiring.

1. Reread the introductory paragraph. What background method is used to introduce the topic? ______________________________

2. Read the thesis statement. Is it general or specific?

   ____

   What will the essay discuss? ______________________________

   ____

3. What three reactions does the writer present in the body paragraphs?

   Body paragraph 1 ______________________________

   Body paragraph 2 ______________________________

   Body paragraph 3 ______________________________

4. Read the sentences below from the essay. Which coherence method (repetition of key terms, pronoun, synonym) is being used in each example?

   a. "While the hourglass is not a classic piece of art, this small, simple mechanism carries with it much power." ______________

   b. "Time is passing, and I can see it. . . . I cannot escape time."

   ____

5. Reread body paragraph 4. The author uses many adjectives in discussing the hourglass. Write five (5) of these adjectives here.

   ____

   ____

   ____

   ____

   ____

6. In the concluding paragraph, what does the author re-state about her reaction to the photo of the hourglass? ______________

   ____

   ____

   ____

   ____

Blueprint Reaction Essay 2: A Reaction to Dylan Thomas' "Do Not Go Gentle into that Good Night"

PREREADING DISCUSSION QUESTIONS

1. *Do you enjoy reading poetry?*
2. *What are your feelings about death? Do you accept it easily? Are you afraid of it?*

EXERCISE 5

Reading and Answering Questions

Read the following poem and essay. Then answer the questions.

DO NOT GO GENTLE INTO THAT GOOD NIGHT
by Dylan Thomas

Dylan Thomas

Do not go gentle into that good night,
Old age should burn and rave at close of day;
Rage, rage against the dying of the light.

Though wise men at their end know dark is right,
Because their words had forked no lightning they
Do not go gentle into that good night.

Good men, the last wave by, crying how bright
Their frail deeds might have danced in a green bay,
Rage, rage against the dying of the light.

Wild men who caught and sang the sun in flight,
And learn, too late, they grieved it on its way,
Do not go gentle into that good night.

Grave men, near death, who see with blinding sight
Blind eyes could blaze like meteors and be gay,
Rage, rage against the dying of the light.

And you, my father, there on the sad height,
Curse, bless, me now with your fierce tears, I pray.
Do not go gentle into that good night.
Rage, rage against the dying of the light.

A Reaction to Dylan Thomas' "Do Not Go Gentle into that Good Night"

1 One of the most well-known poems by Dylan Thomas is "Do Not Go Gentle into that Good Night." Thomas' father had been suffering from throat cancer, and Thomas wrote this poem on the eve of his father's death. "Do Not Go Gentle into that Good Night" is the cry of a man who does not want to see his father die. In the six stanzas of the poem, Thomas examines how different types of people deal with death. He explains their struggles and at the same asks his father to fight death. Thomas' poem is a testament to struggle and a plea to his father not to give in to death. In reading this poem, my feeling is that all people should fight against the **inevitability** of death.

inevitability: impossibility of avoiding or preventing

(continued)

(continued)

futility: hopelessness

regardless: despite; anyway

circumvent: avoid

uneventful: unimportant; boring

readily: easily; willingly

mortality: death; fatality

discriminate: see clear differences

2 Thomas writes that wise men who know that they will experience death fight it. They are aware of the **futility** of trying to continue living, but they attempt to hold on to life. I believe this fight occurs because they feel that they have not done enough good deeds yet. These wise men want to contribute more to society, but death will take them **regardless** of their battle to **circumvent** it.

3 Good, simple men are also known to battle death. Their lives have probably been **uneventful** compared to the lives of the wise men who spent their lives teaching others. However, neither do these people accept death so **readily.** How often do we hear of an average person, a hard-working soul, who struggles to the bitter end of a long illness? It is these common men who routinely show their strength at the end of their lives, but they never win the battle in the end.

4 The third group of men mentioned in the poem is wild men with courage to do and try things that others cannot or will not do. In my opinion, these are the people who fight against death the hardest. Adventurers like these often do not realize their own **mortality.** In these cases, I believe the shock of death in a wild man's eyes is much stronger than in others'.

5 Thomas also includes grave men who battle against death. The serious people who go about their lives without experiencing much pleasure do not want to die. I find this ironic, for why would serious or critical people, perhaps unhappy, want to continue living? These are the souls who are most likely to anticipate death, not fight it. However, Thomas includes them here with all other people who come to a realization before death that they do not want to leave this earth.

6 Death is something that all of us must confront sooner or later. In "Do Not Go Gentle into that Good Night," Dylan Thomas is reminding us that it is human nature to fight the inevitable. Death does not **discriminate** against anyone, yet the human reaction to it is mainly one of resistance.

POSTREADING QUESTIONS

1. *Reread the introductory paragraph. What background method is used to introduce the material?* ______________________

2. *What is the thesis statement of this essay? Write it here.* ______________________

____

3. *What is the general topic of this essay?* ______________________

____

4. *The controlling idea of a topic sentence is the idea that will be discussed in the paragraph. Write the controlling idea in each body paragraph.*

   a. ____________________

   b. ____________________

   c. ____________________

   d. ____________________

5. *Synonyms are often used in essays to enhance coherence. Read the vocabulary words in the chart. Refer to the essay and fill in the synonym column.*

Vocabulary word	**Synonym**
(paragraph 2) fight	
(paragraph 3) battle	
(paragraph 5) grave	

6. *Pronouns are also used to add coherence. Reread paragraph 2. Circle the pronouns that refer to "wise men." Underline the pronouns that refer to the word "death."*

7. *Read the concluding paragraph. What is the author's final opinion about the poem?*

   ____

   ____

   ____

   ____

   ____

   ____

Grammar Focus and Sentence Check

Grammar Focus: Word Forms

The most common parts of speech in English are *nouns, verbs, adjectives,* and *adverbs.* As you learn vocabulary and practice its variations, or word forms, you will advance your writing that much more.

1. *Nouns.* A noun is a person, place, thing, or idea. Some examples are *father, shore, computer, generosity.* Many words can be made into nouns by adding a suffix. A list of common noun suffixes follows.

   -ance, -ence, -or, -er, -ee, -ist, -ism, -ship, -tion, -sion, -ness, -hood, -dom, -ity, -ian

   Examples: Coopera*tion* in the neighbor*hood* for crime watch was at an all-time high.

   Two of our local politic*ians* were recently accused of embezzling funds.

2. *Verbs.* A verb is any type of action or state of being, such as *jump* and *be.*

   Here are some common verb suffixes.

   -ify, -ize, -en, -ate

   Examples: In order to height*en* his awareness of literature, Bob initi*ated* a literature club at his high school.

   The media tends to politic*ize* many events, even if they are not necessarily political in nature.

3. *Adjectives.* An adjective modifies a noun. Typical adjective suffixes include:

   -able, -ible, -al, -tial, -ful, -ous, -tive, -less, -some, -ish

   Examples: Lisa's child*ish* prank in the classroom made her teacher furi*ous.*

   The politic*al* activists were arrested last weekend during the protest march.

4. *Adverbs.* An adverb *modifies* a verb or an adjective. Many adverbs are formed by adding *–ly* to an adjective.

   Examples: Bryant sang wonderful*ly* at the concert last night.

   Personally, Brendan Svenson is a fine man; political*ly,* he doesn't have the experience to succeed in office.

EXERCISE

Finding Word Forms in Essays

Study the word forms below. Refer to Blueprint essay 1 (p. 150) and Blueprint essay 2 (pp. 152–153) to find the missing word forms. The first one is done for you.

NOUN	VERB	ADJECTIVE	ADVERB
Blueprint essay 1			
1. simplicity	simplify	simple	simply
2. persistence	persist	persistent	
3.	x	historical	historically
4.	create	creative	creatively
5. appreciation		appreciative	x
6. smoothness	smooth	smooth	
7. purity	purify		purely
Blueprint essay 2			
8. logic	x		logically
9.	die	dead/deadly	x
10.	x	inevitable	inevitably
11.	strengthen	strong	strongly
12.	please	pleasant	pleasantly
13. irony	x		ironically
14.	realize	real	really
15. critic/criticism	criticize		critically
16. discrimination		discriminating/ed	x

IMPORTANT NOTE:

If all the sentences in an essay are the same type, the writing can sound dull. For example if they are all a short subject-verb-object pattern (*I read the book.*) or if most of the sentences begin with an introductory time clause (*When I thought about that character*), the essay can sound repetitive and formulaic. Reading aloud is a good way to check if you have sentence variety.

Sentence Check: Sentence Variety

To write a well-crafted essay, good writers use sentence variety. There are four main ways to create sentence variety: *coordination, subordination, use of relative pronouns in subordination,* and *use of prepositional phrases.*

1. *Coordination.* Coordination connects two sets of ideas (clauses, sentences, or phrases) using these coordinating conjunctions: *and, but, or, nor, yet, for,* and *so.*

   Original sentences: The firefighters arrived on the scene in only five minutes. The fire was out of control by that time.

   Combined sentence: The firefighters arrived on the scene in only five minutes**, but** the fire was out of control by that time.

2. *Subordination.* Subordination links two sentences that are related. One of the sentences is the main idea, or independent clause, and the other takes on a subordinate (minor) role. Some common connectors used for subordination are: *after, because, before, even if, if, since, though, until, when, while, where.*

   Original sentences: The economic summit was postponed. Three key players could not attend.

   Combined sentence: The economic summit was postponed **because** three key players could not attend.

3. *Use of Relative Pronouns in Subordination.* Relative pronouns combine two clauses into one sentence. The subordinate clause begins with a relative pronoun and describes the independent clause. Common relative pronouns are *which, who, whoever, whom, that, whose.*

   Original sentences: My uncle owns a fine dining restaurant. The restaurant is always full.

   Combined sentence: My uncle owns a fine dining restaurant **that** is always full.

4. *Use of Prepositional Phrases.* A prepositional phrase adds information to the sentence. Some prepositions are *in, on, from, for, with, among, to, at.*

   Original sentences: We heard a frightening noise. The noise came from the attic.

   Combined sentence: We heard a frightening noise **from** the attic.

EXERCISE 7

Sentence Variety

Read the excerpts from Blueprint essay 1 (p. 150) and Blueprint essay 2 (pp. 152–153). Underline and label the sentence variety elements that occur in each excerpt: coordination (C), subordination (S), relative pronouns (RP), and prepositional phrases (PP). (Hint: Look for at least two examples in each excerpt.) The first one is done for you.

C PP

1. Time is passing, and I can see it. It is right there in front of me.
2. I cannot lie to myself and tell myself that I will do what I need to do tomorrow or the next day.
3. I had better hurry up and do something with my life before the grains of sand have all fallen through the crevice.
4. The poem is the cry of a man who does not want to see his father die.
5. This fight occurs because they feel that they have not done enough good deeds yet. These wise men want to contribute more, but death will take them anyway.

EXERCISE

Editing Practice: Grammar Focus and Sentence Check Application

Read this paragraph carefully. Find and correct the six errors in word forms. The first one is done for you.

Whenever I see a store window decorated with Christmas trees and Santa Claus, I experience a variety of feelings. The first emotion that comes to me is one of ~~happy.~~ happiness This time of year, especially in my country, is filled with love, joyful, and hope for the future. People seem friendlier and more kindness. This emotion, however, sometimes gives way to another more negative one. I feel disgusted, cheated, and materialistic. By letting myself get caught up in the frenetic rush to spend money, I cheap the holiday itself. I wish I could ignore the ads and go with my feel, to be closely with my family and enjoy this season. Maybe it will happen next year.

PART B

The Writing Process: Practice Writing a Reaction Essay

Objectives	In Part B, you will:
Prewriting:	use your eyes "as a camera"
Planning:	combine descriptions and reactions in a chart
Partner Feedback:	review classmates' charts and analyze feedback
First Draft:	write a reaction essay use background information in the essay
Partner Feedback:	review classmates' essays and analyze feedback
Final Draft:	use feedback to write a final draft of your reaction essay

The Writing Process: Writing Assignment

Your assignment is to write a reaction to a photo. Study the photo below. What do you see? How does it make you feel? Does it remind you of anything you have seen in real life or in your field of study? Follow the steps in the writing process in this section.

Prewriting: Using Your Eyes as a Camera

When you react to a visual prompt, you need to convey to the reader a strong impression of what you are looking at, so it is important to begin with a vivid description. By focusing on description, you not only brainstorm information to put in the background of the essay, but you also get a feeling for the reaction you will produce in the rest of the essay.

EXERCISE

Describing Images

Imagine that your eyes are a wandering camera. Look at all aspects of the photo on p. 159. How many images do you see? How is the lighting in the photo? What are the textures? What actions are happening? Fill in the chart below.

WHAT DO YOU SEE?

Object	Description	Actions	Light	Texture

EXERCISE **10**

Generating Personal Reaction

1. Based on the descriptions you noted in the chart in Exercise 8 and a review of the photo on p. 159, summarize your main reaction in a sentence or two.

____

____

2. Now break down your main reaction into three or four smaller, related feelings. Fill in the blanks in the chart. Keep referring back to the photo on p. 159 as you work.

Emotion 1	
Emotion 2	
Emotion 3	
Emotion 4	

EXERCISE **11**

Brainstorming Supporting Information

In **column 1** *below, write each of the emotions you wrote in Exercise 10. Then fill in* **column 2** *with words and ideas that explain or relate to the emotion. You will use this information as supporting details in your body paragraphs.*

Emotions	**Details**
1.	
2.	
3.	
4.	

Planning: Combining Descriptions and Reactions

Now that you have described the illustration and explained your feelings about it, you are ready to plan how all this information will appear in an essay. Begin with description, then organize the body paragraphs, each dealing with one emotion. Use the chart to organize your essay.

EXERCISE 12

Charting Your Essay Information

Combine the information you generated in Exercises 9, 10, and 11 into the chart below and add introductory and concluding information. Except for the thesis statement, you do not have to write complete sentences. Follow these steps.

1. For the introductory paragraph, add some descriptive notes about the photo.
2. Write a thesis statement that tells your main reaction to the photo and indicates what you will discuss in the essay.
3. Choose the emotions that you will discuss in each body paragraph. What supporting details will you include?
4. Write notes about a final, summarizing opinion of the photo.

Introductory description	
Thesis statement	
Body paragraphs	1. 2. 3.
Concluding ideas	

Partner Feedback Form 1

Exchange outlines with another student. Read your partner's outline and answer the questions on Partner Feedback Form 1: Unit 6, p. 239, in Appendix 3. Discuss your partner's reactions to your outline. Make notes about any parts you need to change before you write your paper. For more information about giving partner feedback, see Appendix 2, p. 218, Guidelines for Partner Feedback.

First Draft

You are now ready to write the first draft of your essay. Before you begin, review your chart from Exercise 12 and any comments from your partner.

EXERCISE 13

Writing the Introduction

Write an introduction for your topic, using your chart and the feedback you received from your partner. Use description as background information in your introduction to begin your essay (see p. 147). "The Hourglass and Me" on p. 150 uses this type of introductory information. You can use it as a model if you want. End your introduction with a well-constructed thesis statement. When you finish, use the checklist to review your work.

Introduction Checklist

	YES	NO
▸ Did I use effective background information in the form of description?	❑	❑
▸ Do I avoid writing my personal reaction to the illustration in my introduction—waiting until the thesis?	❑	❑
▸ Does my thesis statement provide the reader with a clear guide that the essay will discuss my reaction to the illustration?	❑	❑
▸ Is the purpose of my essay clear?	❑	❑

What is it? ________________________________

EXERCISE 14

Writing Body Paragraphs

Look again at your introductory paragraph and the ***charts*** *you created to plan your reaction essay. Then write the body paragraphs. When you finish, use the checklist to review your work.*

IMPORTANT NOTE:

One important thing to consider when you write a reaction essay is to use personal feelings in your body paragraphs. In this type of writing, it is appropriate to use the first person singular, *I*.

Body Paragraph Checklist

	YES	NO
▸ Does each body paragraph treat only one main emotion or reaction?	❑	❑
▸ Does each contain a topic sentence with a clear controlling idea?	❑	❑
▸ Does each paragraph end with a logical concluding sentence?	❑	❑
▸ Do my body paragraphs all relate to and support the thesis statement of the essay? In other words, does each address part of my reaction?	❑	❑
▸ Do I repeat important key terms?	❑	❑

(continued)

Body Paragraph Checklist (continued)

	YES	NO
▸ Do I use pronouns to help my writing flow coherently?	❑	❑
▸ Do I use synonyms for key words in my body paragraphs?	❑	❑
▸ Are all the word forms correct?	❑	❑
▸ Do I use sentence variety?	❑	❑
▸ Are all sentences in my body paragraphs relevant to the topic? That is, do they have unity?	❑	❑

EXERCISE 15

WRITING A CONCLUSION

Review again your chart, introduction, and body. Write a concluding paragraph for your essay. When you finish, use the checklist to review your work.

Conclusion Checklist

	YES	NO
▸ Does my conclusion successfully signal the end of my essay?	❑	❑
▸ Does my conclusion add coherence to the essay by:		
a. restating the essay thesis?	❑	❑
b. summarizing or restating the essay subtopics?	❑	❑
▸ Does my conclusion:		
a. leave the reader with my final thoughts?	❑	❑
b. offer a final, summarizing opinion about my reaction to the illustration?	❑	❑

Partner Feedback Form 2

Exchange essays with another student. Read your partner's essay and answer the questions on Partner Feedback Form 2: Unit 6, pp. 241–242, in Appendix 3. Discuss your partner's reactions to your essay. Make notes about any parts you need to change before you write your second draft. For more information about giving partner feedback, see Appendix 2, p. 218, Guidelines for Partner Feedback.

Final Draft

Carefully revise your essay using all the feedback you have received: partner review of your chart and essay, instructor comments, and any evaluation you have done yourself. Use the checklist to do a final check of your essay. In addition, try reading your essay aloud. This can help you find awkward-sounding sentences and errors in punctuation. When you finish, add a title to your essay and neatly type your final draft. See Appendix 4, p. 246, for information about writing titles.

Final Draft Checklist

	YES	NO
▸ Did I use an effective description to introduce the illustration I am reacting to?	❑	❑
▸ Did I include a thesis statement that contains a clear topic and controlling idea?	❑	❑
▸ Did I focus my reaction on my feelings and thoughts?	❑	❑
▸ Did I use the first person "I" in my body paragraphs to explain my reaction?	❑	❑
▸ Did I create coherence by		
a. repeating key nouns in my body paragraphs?	❑	❑
b. replacing some nouns with pronouns?	❑	❑
c. using synonyms for some key vocabulary to avoid sounding repetitive?	❑	❑
▸ Have I used sentence variety and correct word forms?	❑	❑
▸ Are all my topic sentences clear and focused?	❑	❑
▸ Does my concluding paragraph successfully signal the end of my essay and sound like a final paragraph?	❑	❑
▸ Does my essay have unity and coherence?	❑	❑

Additional Writing Assignments from the Academic Disciplines

Beginning with the Prewriting activity on p. 160, use the writing process and write another essay. Choose a topic from the following list.

SUBJECT	*WRITING TASK*
Entertainment	Write a reaction essay about a film you have recently seen. Summarize the film's plot in the introduction. How did you feel about the film? Could you identify with the situation? How do you evaluate the film?

SUBJECT	*WRITING TASK*
Politics	Write a reaction to the concept of Marxism. First summarize or explain Marxism, then react to it as a concept. What does it mean to you? Do you agree with its philosophy? Why or why not?
Literature	Write a reaction essay about a short story. In the introductory paragraph, summarize the plot of the story. How does the story relate to your life? What are your feelings about what you read? What significance does the story have for you?
Lecture Analysis	Write a reaction to a lecture you have recently attended. Include a brief summary. What did you know about the topic prior to listening to the lecture? How does your experience add to the information you learned? What is your reaction to the topic and the instructor's delivery style?

UNIT 7

Blueprints for

ARGUMENTATIVE ESSAYS

PART A

Blueprints for Argumentative Essays

Objectives	**In Part A, you will:**
Analysis:	study the structure of argumentative essays
Unity and Coherence:	
Unity:	learn how to take only one stance
Coherence: Transition Expressions	learn to use *although it may be true that/despite the fact that, certainly,* and *surely*
Grammar Focus:	study prepositions
Sentence Check:	study noun clauses
Practice:	determine the opposing sides of an issue and use different methods of organization

What Is an Argumentative Essay?

Writers choose argumentative essays when they want to persuade readers to change their minds about something. In this kind of essay, writers must convince readers of their point of view.

IMPORTANT NOTE:

Often argumentative essays include some of the other types of writing discussed in *Blueprints*. For example, you may want to *compare and contrast* (Unit 4) the opposing views in your essay to show the reader why your view is the best one. Or, to illustrate your point that a diet low in cholesterol can prevent heart disease, you might explain the *process* (Unit 3) of how cholesterol develops into plaque in coronary arteries. You will study more about using these and other methods later in this unit.

Developing an Argumentative Essay

The word "issue" is frequently used to describe a problem situation in which there are differing points of view. To argue about an issue, you must first discover all the different sides of the issue and which viewpoints you agree with. Then, you must clearly understand *what the opposing viewpoint is.* It is helpful to first state your viewpoint in a direct and clear manner. Then take the opposite position: what is that viewpoint? Stating the opposing viewpoint will help you clearly identify an opponent's position, which you will need to address in your essay.

EXERCISE 1

Determining the Opposing Viewpoints

Determine the opposing viewpoints for each of the following statements. Write the viewpoints in the blanks. The first one is done for you.

1. Early childhood education programs prevent later criminal activity.
   Early childhood education programs have no impact on later criminal activity.
2. Parents should impose rules for their teenage children about the use of the Internet.
   should not
3. Doctors and nurses do not provide adequate pain management for terminally ill patients.
4. Marijuana use for medical purposes should not be legalized in the United States.
5. It is perfectly ethical to accept donations from pharmaceutical companies to conduct scientific research at universities.

Once you choose a side to defend and state the opposite argument, you can develop your argument by *creating a list of reasons for your viewpoint.*

EXERCISE 2

Supporting Ideas

For each main argument, think of two different supporting ideas to back it up. Write your ideas after each statement. The first one is done for you.

1. Columbus Day should not be celebrated as a holiday in the United States.
   a. Columbus did not really "discover" America.
   b. Columbus slaughtered and enslaved native people.

2. Spanking is harmful to children.

   a. ____

   b. ____

3. A vegetarian diet is healthier than one that includes meat.

   a. ____

   b. ____

4. One parent should care for children full time until they begin school.

   a. ____

   b. ____

5. The government should not prevent genetic cloning of human organs for medical purposes.

   a. ____

   b. ____

Introductions in Argumentative Essays

To begin your argumentative essay, you can use any of the introductory techniques already presented in *Blueprints 2,* including turning an argument on its head (explained in Unit 1, p. 17, and later in this unit on page 195). No matter which technique you use, your first paragraph needs to include the following:

- a brief explanation of the issue (This can include background information to help the reader understand what the topic is all about.)
- a clear statement of both sides of the issue
- an argumentative thesis statement, which is distinctive in that it takes a stand on the issue

Methods of Organization for Argumentative Essays

There are three common methods of organizing an argumentative essay. No one method is better than another; each one provides a different way of organizing the details of your argument and countering the opposing viewpoint. What is important to know is that following any one of these methods of organization will provide order and logic to your essay. Review the chart below. Note that you may have more or fewer details and arguments in your essay than you see here.

Method 1	**Method 2**	**Method 3**
1. Introduction a. Explanation of the issue (Use an introductory technique, such as turning an argument on its head.) b. Statement of both sides of the issue c. Argumentative thesis statement 2. Argument 1 for your stance a. Detail 1 b. Detail 2 c. Etc. 3. Argument 2 for your stance a. Detail 1 b. Detail 2 c. Etc. 4. Argument 3 for your stance a. Detail 1 b. Detail 2 c. Etc. 5. Counter-argument a. Statement of the opposing view b. Refutation of opposing view 1 c. Refutation of opposing view 2 d. Etc. 6. Conclusion a. Detail 1 b. Detail 2 c. Etc.	1. Introduction a. Explanation of the issue (Use an introductory technique, such as turning an argument on its head.) b. Statement of both sides of the issue c. Argumentative thesis statement 2. Refute the opposing stance with Argument 1 a. Statement of the opposing stance b. Detail 1 c. Detail 2 d. Etc. 3. Refute the opposing stance with Argument 2 a. Detail 1 b. Detail 2 c. Etc. 4. Refute the opposing stance with Argument 3 a. Detail 1 b. Detail 2 c. Etc. 5. Conclusion a. Detail 1 b. Detail 2 c. Etc.	1. Introduction a. Explanation of the issue (Use an introductory technique, such as turning an argument on its head.) b. Statement of both sides of the issue c. Argumentative thesis statement 2. Counter-argument a. Statement of the opposing view b. Refutation of opposing view 1 c. Refutation of opposing view 2 d. Etc. 3. Argument 1 for your stance (weakest) a. Detail 1 b. Detail 2 c. Etc. 4. Argument 2 for your stance (stronger) a. Detail 1 b. Detail 2 c. Etc. 5. Argument 3 for your stance (strongest) a. Detail 1 b. Detail 2 c. Etc. 6. Conclusion a. Detail 1 b. Detail 2 c. Etc.

Unity in Argumentative Essays

While you may understand more than one viewpoint about an issue, it is important to argue for only one viewpoint in your essay. Otherwise you might weaken your argument and your essay will lack unity. For example, you can confuse your reader if you stray from one position. You might even lend credibility to other views if you don't stay focused on one viewpoint.

Taking only one stance (viewpoint) in an argument helps you achieve **unity.** For example, if you argue against the death penalty but then assert that it is acceptable in some cases, you provide an opening for those who would argue for it in many more circumstances. This opposing viewpoint would discredit your argument (See Unit 1, pp. 4–5 and 21–22 for more about unity in essays.)

EXERCISE 3

Sticking to One Stance

One of the supporting statements listed for each viewpoint does not relate to the argument. Cross out the statement that does not belong in the list. The first one is done for you.

1. Television adversely affects children.
   a. Children who watch longs hours of television do not read often enough.
   b. School performance goes down when children spend many hours watching television
   ~~c. Some educational television programs help children who are visually oriented learn better.~~
2. The mounting body of science proving that manmade greenhouse gases trap heat in the earth's atmosphere is convincing more and more people that we must cut greenhouse pollution drastically.
   a. Global warming in coastal states like Florida will lead to flooding and saltwater contamination of underground drinking water supplies.
   b. More frequent wildfires and declining crop yields are only two of the consequences of global warming.
   c. This paper seeks to assist policymakers and the public in better understanding the institutional resistance to efforts to curb greenhouse pollution.
3. Exposure to the sun for long periods can cause skin cancer.
   a. There is a direct connection between skin cancer and chronic exposure to the sun.
   b. A history of sunburns is correlated with skin cancer later in life.
   c. Exposure to sunlight is an important source of Vitamin D, a vital nutrient.
4. Alexander the Great was considered one of the finest kings of the western world.
   a. Although he brutally conquered many people, Alexander often encouraged the intermarriage of his own Macedonians and the women who survived his conquests.

b. Alexander opened routes for trade and communication between the eastern and western worlds.

c. Alexander's religious tolerance earned him the respect of many people around the world.

5. The benefits of space exploration are worth the costs.

a. As natural resources needed for human survival are depleted, new sources may be found on other planets and moons.

b. Eventually, to alleviate overcrowding on Earth, humans will need to settle on other planets.

c. Most of our knowledge of the solar system comes from ground-based observations and Earth-orbiting satellites.

Coherence in Argumentative Essays

As discussed in previous units, the use of well-placed transition expressions is among the most important practices for adding coherence to paragraphs and essays. In addition to the transition expressions you have already learned, the ones below are especially useful for argumentative writing.

Transition Expressions

Transition Expressions: *although it may be true that/despite the fact that, certainly,* and *surely*

although it may be true that/despite the fact that

Function: to say that something is true before saying something else about it

Use: *Although it may be true that* and *despite that* are used to concede a point that supports the opposing argument. These transition expressions are followed by a clause that introduces the opposing view.

Examples: **Although it may be true that** there appear to be dry riverbeds on the planet Mars, this does not prove that water or life once existed there.

Despite the fact that the shortest distance between two points is a straight line, you cannot often drive or walk in a straight line to your destination.

Punctuation Note: *Although it may be true that/despite the fact that* + clause that states the opposing view is followed by a comma before stating your stance in a separate clause.

(continued)

(continued)

certainly

Function: to say that the writer agrees with something without any doubt

Use: *Certainly* is an adverb used in argumentative writing to lend credibility to the writer's stance.

Examples: **Certainly** one would not wish to risk the lives of innocent people by driving recklessly.

The new regime will **certainly** take over the formerly private industry to make it publicly controlled.

surely

Function: implies that the writer has faith in the statement that follows

Use: *Surely* is an adverb used to express certainty. It differs slightly from *certainly* in that *surely* expresses more urgency and persuasion.

Examples: **Surely** if the banks run into trouble, the Federal Reserve should lower interest rates again.

Nuclear power plants **surely** represent the most efficient energy sources for today's needs.

Blueprints Argumentative Essays

In this section, you will read and analyze two sample argumentative essays. These essays can act as blueprints when you write your own argumentative essay in Part B.

Blueprint Argumentative Essay 1: Why Adopt a Vegetarian Diet?

PREREADING DISCUSSION QUESTIONS

1. *Do you know anyone who is a vegetarian? Do you know why that person is a vegetarian?*
2. *Why do you think most vegetarians choose not to eat meat?*

EXERCISE 4

Reading and Answering Questions

Read the argumentative essay. Fill in the blanks with transition expressions from the list. Then answer the postreading questions.

although it may be true that surely certainly

Why Adopt a Vegetarian Diet?

1 "Meat and potatoes" is a phrase used in American English that means the centerpiece of a meal. Besides referring to food, "meat" signifies the most important part of anything. It has been such a deeply **ingrained,** time-honored tradition for families to build a meal around meat, that one can safely say that meat has become the heart of an American meal. Meat gives us protein, and therefore, our strength. However, this widely held belief that meat is necessary for health and vitality has outlived its usefulness. While some people continue to hold onto this outdated perception of the importance of meat, others are letting go of it and becoming vegetarian. That is, Americans are correcting their beliefs about meat and increasingly becoming vegetarian for **ethical,** environmental, and health reasons.

ingrained: thoroughly filled, as with an idea in the mind

2 One reason for becoming vegetarian is to prevent cruelty to animals. Animals, like humans, feel pain, stress, and fear. People cannot morally justify the pain and suffering of animals that are killed for food when **adequate** nutrition can be found in plant foods. Not only do animals experience these physical sensations when they are needlessly slaughtered for human **consumption,** but they are often treated cruelly prior to slaughter. Veal calves, for example, are forced to live in extremely small cages no longer than their bodies so they cannot move and create unwanted muscle. They are then killed when they are just twelve to sixteen weeks old so that their weak, immature muscles will produce soft meat.

ethical: behaving within accepted boundaries of right and wrong

adequate: enough to satisfy a requirement or need

consumption: the act of eating or drinking

3 In addition to ethical reasons, some vegetarians choose not to eat meat for environmental reasons. Cattle production, for example, is a major cause of soil **erosion** due to overgrazing of land, which creates deserts out of grasslands. Cattle production also creates water pollution through **organic waste** and the use of chemicals in animal feed. In addition, cattle production pollutes the air. Grain-fed cattle contribute significantly to global warming through the production of carbon dioxide, methane,

erosion: a process by which material is worn away from the earth's surface

organic waste: undigested food residue from living animals

(continued)

(continued)

and nitrous oxide. The burning of the world's forests for cattle pasture has released billions of tons of carbon dioxide into the **atmosphere.** The world's cattle release millions of tons of methane through their digestive systems directly into the atmosphere each year. Moreover, producing feed crops for cattle involves the use of petro-chemical fertilizers, which **emit** vast amounts of nitrous oxide. These gases are building up in the atmosphere, blocking heat from escaping the planet, and could cause **cataclysmic** global climate changes in this century.

atmosphere: the mass of gas surrounding a planet, especially Earth

emit: to give or send out matter or energy

cataclysmic: causing a violent upheaval with great destruction

4 While some vegetarians make the choice not to eat meat for ethical and environmental reasons, others are concerned with personal health. The health benefits of not eating meat are undisputed, even among the most traditional and conservative medical doctors today. In scientific studies, vegetarian diets are **correlated** with lower **cholesterol** levels, lower rates of heart disease, high blood pressure, obesity, diabetes, and colon cancer. As a result, vegetarians tend to live longer, healthier lives.

correlated: related in a parallel or interchangeable way

cholesterol: a white crystalline substance, $C_{27}H_{45}HO$; part of what makes cell membranes fluid

counter

5 Some fear that not eating meat will be difficult for nutritional, cultural, and practical reasons, but these fears can be easily **allayed.** Because meat, poultry, or fish is traditionally the focal point of meals, some people think meals are inadequate without a large portion of protein on the table, with vegetables downgraded to secondary roles. ____________________ most meat-eating Americans get the bulk of their iron, protein, and vitamin B12 from meat sources, people can easily get **ample** amounts of these nutrients from a varied diet that includes nuts, seeds, and grains. Even vegans, who eat no animal products at all, can take a daily vitamin and mineral supplement to bolster iron and vitamin B12 intake. Most restaurants now cater to vegetarians, especially ethnic restaurants like Mexican, Italian, and Indian, making it easy to be vegetarian and eat out. Even when there are no vegetarian choices on the menu, most chefs will ____________________ be happy to **oblige** when asked to produce a special vegetarian meal. Finally, when faced with family food traditions that involve meat eating,

allayed: reduced the intensity of; calmed

ample: more than enough, fully sufficient for a purpose

oblige: to do a service or favor for

(continued)

(continued)

such as Thanksgiving, most vegetarians can ask the cook for a nonmeat choice ahead of time or may bring a vegetable dish of their own.

6 For most vegetarians, the choice to become vegetarian is not taken lightly. ______________________, if one was not brought up as a child to abstain from eating meat, the switch to vegetarianism means a change in deeply ingrained eating habits. The benefits of vegetarianism to animals, to the environment, and most of all to personal health, however, far outweigh the small inconvenience people might feel for a week or so after beginning a nonmeat diet. For all vegetarians, eating a flesh-free diet is a decision made for important global or personal reasons that not only impact personal health and well being, but also the health and well being of the planet. In the not-too-distant future, the phrase "meat and potatoes" will become a relic of the past, just like the **antiquated** belief in the need for a carnivorous diet.

antiquated: old-fashioned; out of date

Some parts adapted from http://www.mcspotlight.org/media/reports/beyond.html—April 24, 2001

POSTREADING DISCUSSION QUESTIONS

1. *What is the thesis statement of this essay? Write it here.*

   Amilecans . . . reasons.

2. *What introduction technique is used in this essay? (See Unit 1, pp. 15–17 for a list of introductory techniques.)*

   quotation method

3. *What method of organization is used in this essay? (See Methods of Organization for Argumentative Essays on p. 171)*

   ____

4. *What point is the writer arguing in this essay?*

   about being vegetarian dice

5. *What point of view is the opposite of what the writer is saying?*

you can't take your daily nut... from veg

6. *Write down each reason the writer gives to support the argument.*

Reason 1: ______

Reason 2: ______

Reason 3: ______

7. *In an argumentative essay, the writer must address the viewpoint of the opposing argument. List the three opposing points that are taken up in this essay.*

Point 1: ______

Point 2: ______

Point 3: ______

8. *Underline the controlling idea of each body paragraph in the essay. Does each body paragraph address only one of the subtopics?*

______

9. *Does the writer convince you of his viewpoint?* yes. *If not, why not?*

______

10. *Does the conclusion provide a summary of the main points of the argument?* maybe.

Blueprint Argumentative Essay 2: **Coffee: Surprising Benefits from This Herbal Supplement**

PREREADING DISCUSSION QUESTIONS

1. *Have you ever drunk coffee to stay up late to write a paper?*
2. *Do you think that coffee is good for you or bad for you? Why?*
3. *What are the benefits of drinking coffee? Are there any?*
4. *Do you think coffee has any medicinal value?*

EXERCISE 5

Reading and Answering Questions

Read the argumentative essay. Fill in the blanks with transition expressions from the list. Then answer the postreading questions.

surely despite the fact that certainly

Coffee: Surprising Benefits from This Herbal Supplement

purported: given a false appearance

enhances: makes something greater or of more value

1 People everywhere are trying to cut back on their consumption of this "harmful" drink, all the while craving coffee desperately and feeling guilty when they indulge. Coffee is said to cause nervousness and is **purported** to be addictive. We have all heard about these harmful effects of coffee, but many Americans continue to drink it daily. What if instead of feeling guilty about drinking coffee, you could feel good about taking this herbal supplement? Consider these facts: coffee combats drowsiness, temporarily boosts athletic performance, eases congestion due to colds and flu, prevents asthma attacks, and **enhances** the pain-relieving effects of aspirin. Research on the benefits of coffee shows that it deserves our respect as an important supplement.

unsubstantiated: not established by proof or competent evidence

constituent: an essential part

2 Over the years, many attempts have been made to associate coffee with negative health effects. However, these claims remain **unsubstantiated.** ______________________ coffee can cause sleeplessness and nervousness, this is true only when it is drunk in large doses. The medically important **constituent** of coffee is caffeine, but the caffeine content of coffee depends on how it is prepared. A cup of instant coffee contains about 60 milligrams of caffeine, whereas a cup of drip, percolated or even espresso coffee has about 100 milligrams. Most doctors say that coffee appears to pose no particular threat to most people if it is consumed in moderation. According to new research presented at the national meeting of the American Chemical Society, coffee is not very addictive. French researchers reported that caffeine has no effect on the area of the brain involved with addiction at doses of one to three cups of coffee per day. Astrid Nehlig, Ph.D. of the French National Health and Medical Research Institute conducted research on coffee consumption with laboratory animals. This research confirmed that while moderate does of caffeine contribute to increased alertness and energy, dependence does not occur at those levels.

(continued)

(continued)

3 ________________________ coffee is best known as the powerful stimulant that helps people stay awake during night driving and cramming before final exams. Its caffeine is capable of boosting energy, increasing alertness, and quickening reaction time. It is also a mood elevator and may help mild depression. The explanation for this may lie in research conducted in the mid-1980s, which suggested that the **chlorogenic acids** in coffee might have an antidepressant effect on the opiate system in the brain. Recently, researchers from the University of Bristol reviewed a decade of research into caffeine's influence on **cognition** and mood. The survey revealed that a cup of coffee could help in the performance of tasks requiring sustained attention, even during low alertness situations such as after lunch, at night, or when a person has a cold.

chlorogenic acid: $C_{16}H_{18}O_9$, a substance that forms around infected tissue in some higher plants and has anti-fungal properties

cognition: mental ability

4 Coffee's health advantages are not confined to mood elevation and increased energy; there are more specific benefits as well for colds, asthma, athletic performance and pain relief. Some over-the-counter cold formulas contain caffeine, partly to counteract the sedative effects of the antihistamines they contain, but caffeine also helps open the bronchial tubes, relieving the congestion of colds and flu. Coffee's action as a **bronchodilator** can also help prevent asthma attacks. In addition, several studies show that, compared with plain aspirin, the combination of aspirin and caffeine relieves pain significantly better than aspirin alone. The reason is caffeine's ability to speed up the body's metabolism so that the aspirin's pain reducing effects are felt faster. Finally, coffee may also improve physical stamina, according to a report published in the journal *The Physician and Sports Medicine.* Athletes who want coffee's benefits typically drink three or four cups during the hour or two before an event.

bronchodilator: a substance that causes expansion of the air spaces of the lungs

5 Although most people don't think of it as such, coffee is ______________________ America's most popular herbal beverage. Despite the scare tactics of those who would try to discredit coffee's reputation, years of research have not shown harmful effects, when coffee is taken in moderation. It not only helps a sleepy nation wake up in the morning, but it also has significant **therapeutic** value, which has been scientifically proven.

therapeutic: acting as a cure or relief

Adapted from http://www.healthyideas.com/healing/herb/coffee.html
Prevention magazine reports, and
http://www.accessexcellence.com/WN/SUA12/cafe399.html,
May 2001

POSTREADING DISCUSSION QUESTIONS

1. *What is the argumentative thesis statement of this essay? Write it here.*

   ____

2. *How many subtopics are there? What are they? Write them here.*

   ____

3. *Does the introductory paragraph include background information about the issue?*

   ____

4. *Does the introduction section include a clear statement of both sides of the issue?*

   ____

5. *Underline the controlling idea of each body paragraph in the essay. Does each body paragraph address one of the subtopics?*

   ____

6. *What one stance is taken on the issue to provide unity?*

   ____

   Is the argument successful? ______________________________

7. *What is the opposing argument?* ______________________________

   ____

8. *Which method of organization is used to develop the argument? (See Methods of Organization for Argumentative Essays on p. 171.)*

   ____

9. *An argumentative essay includes details about each reason offered to support the argument. Often the details are examples. At other times they might be details of a process, causes and effects, comparisons, etc. What is primarily used in this essay to give details about the reasons for the author's view? Circle one.*

   examples   descriptions of a process

   causes and effects   comparisons

   the opinion of experts

10. *Besides signaling the end of the essay, what other purpose does the conclusion fulfill?*

    ____

Grammar Focus and Sentence Check

Grammar Focus: Prepositions

A **preposition** is a word that takes a noun or pronoun object. It often expresses meanings like time, location, or direction. A preposition plus its object is called a **prepositional phrase.**

Examples:

direction	**location**	**time**
to Bangkok	*in* the attic	*after* the storm

Prepositional phrases can occur in several positions in the sentence. Those that express the idea of time are found at the beginning or end of a sentence.

Examples:

During the evening, I stay away from the computer.

I stay away from the computer **during the evening.**

Prepositional phrases that show location or direction occur after the verb and the object of the verb.

Examples:

Cattle release methane **into the atmosphere.**

Students find articles **in scholarly journals.**

Some very common prepositional phrases usually occur with no article. They often refer to everyday activities like eating, sleeping, working, and studying.

at home	*in* school	*to* school
at school	*in* church	*to* church
at church	*in* bed	*to* lunch

Example:

Q: Where's Keith?

A: He's **at school.**

However, when the object of the preposition refers to a specific location (like the building itself), it occurs with an article.

Examples:

Q: Are you going to Keith's party? It's **at the community center.**

A: I'm going **to the community center,** but not **to the party.**

Common prepositional phrases referring to transportation also occur with no article:

by plane/train/car *on* foot

Examples:

I went **by car,** but Lisa went **on foot.**

EXERCISE 6

Prepositional Phrases in *Coffee: Surprising Benefits from This Herbal Supplement*

Reread Blueprint essay 2, "Coffee: Surprising Benefits from This Herbal Supplement."

1. Underline all the prepositional phrases that you can find in this essay.
2. How many prepositional phrases did you find? ______

   Write them here. ______________________________

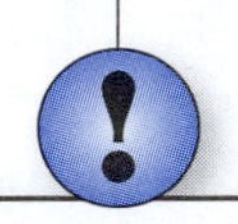

IMPORTANT NOTE:

Infinitives are often mistaken for prepositional phrases. An infinitive is *to* + **the base form of a verb** and functions as a noun.

Examples: Even vegans, who eat no animal products at all, can take a daily vitamin and mineral supplement **to bolster** iron and vitamin B12 intake.

Most doctors say that coffee appears **to pose** no particular threat to most people if it is consumed in moderation.

Prepositional phrases that use *to* often express direction or location.

Examples: The bill, with the chairman's approval, is going **to committee.**

Later, the Dutch brought the coffee plant **to Java.**

EXERCISE 7

Article or No Article?

Decide whether an article is needed as part of the prepositional phrase in each sentence. Circle the correct prepositional phrase.

1. After class, Bill and Omi are going ______ in the cafeteria.
   a. to lunch b. to the lunch
2. Masako's husband goes ______ after she leaves.
   a. to work b. to the work
3. Harold is not ______ today.
   a. in school b. in the school
4. He's sick, so he stayed home ______.
   a. in bed b. to bed
5. Beth doesn't have a car. She goes everywhere ______.
   a. by the foot b. on foot

EXERCISE 8

Prepositional Phrases in Argumentative Essays

A. Specific prepositions and prepositional phrases can be used in different types of writing as you develop your argument. Study this chart:

Type of Writing	Use of Prepositional Phrases	Examples
Argumentative	To concede (admit) a point made by the opposition	Despite, in spite of + Noun Phrase
Comparison	To compare one thing or idea to another	like + Noun Phrase as + Noun Phrase
Process /Description	To explain the chronological order of events	in, on, at, during, by, until
	To explain the spatial order of things	in, around, from, through, out of

B. Write a preposition in each sentence, using the chart to assist you. Then, following each sentence, decide to which type of writing the sentence belongs. The first one is done for you.

1. Like ________ Christmas, Chanukah is celebrated shortly before the beginning of the new year and involves lighting candles.

   Writing type: comparison ________

2. ________ the warning signals that were sent out by the military, protestors continued their demonstration.

   Writing type: ________

3. ________ the 1960s in the United States, laws that might have protected the civil rights of African Americans were often not enforced.

   Writing type: ________

4. ______________________ the Cold War, much of the world was divided politically in terms of alliance with either the former Soviet Union or the United States.

   Writing type: ______________________________________

5. ______________________ Marx, Comte, and Weber believed in the possibility of using scientific methods to study the behavior of people in groups.

   Writing type: ______________________________________

6. ______________________ the fact that the Kyoto Protocol was not signed by the United States, there is still hope for an international response to global warming.

   Writing type: ______________________________________

Sentence Check: Noun Clauses

Noun clauses function like nouns. Like all clauses, a noun clause has a subject and a verb. A noun clause can begin with *that,* a *wh-* word, *if,* or *whether.* These words link a noun clause to the main clause of the sentence.

Main Clause	Noun Clause
It is not certain	**if/whether vegetarianism will increase in popularity.**
They asked	**where Wallace is staying.**
I know	**that coffee helps me wake up in the morning.**

Functions and Rules for Noun Clauses

1. Noun clauses usually function like nouns: they can be subjects, subject complements, objects of verbs, and objects of prepositions. Note that as subjects, noun clauses take singular verbs.

   What you just saw is an incredible facsimile. (subject)

   Their belief is **that agriculture should provide shelter as well as food.** (subject complement)

   I don't know **whether they left yet or not.** (object)

   She looked around **where he lost his keys.** (object of preposition)

2. Noun clauses can also follow some adjectives, such as *certain* and *happy*.

   Trang is certain **that the spring rolls are cooked.**

   The golfers were happy **that the rain stopped.**

3. Noun clauses tend to be used with verbs and adjectives that express mental activity.

   I *decided* **that I don't trust her.**

   He is *positive* **that the door was locked.**

EXERCISE 

Identifying Noun Clauses

Underline the noun clauses in the following sentences. Then rewrite the sentences, substituting a different noun clause in the same place in the sentence. The first one is done for you.

1. Can you tell me if this plane is going to Chicago? Can you tell me if the library will be open till 10:00 tonight?

2. This video shows how coffee beans are processed.

   ____

3. Whether accepting campaign contributions from oil companies is ethical or not is the subject of the debate. ______________

   ____

4. Can you hear which song is playing on the radio right now?

____

5. It doesn't surprise me that you passed the test.

____

Noun Clauses with *That*

1. Noun clauses with *that* can be used after many verbs and adjectives. The word *that* is often omitted.

   Although it may be true **that the television is on,** Kevin has fallen asleep and is not watching it.

   I am sure **(that) the temperature has dropped.**

2. The word *that* cannot be omitted if the noun clause is in the subject position.

   ***That* you are a student** is news to me. **Not:** You are a student is news to me.

3. Although *that* clauses appear in the subject position, more often the word *it* is the subject.

   ***That* you are a student** is news to me. = **It** is news to me **that you are a student.**

4. Noun phrases like *the fact, the idea* and *the possibility* often precede *that* clauses.

   The possibility *that* we can affect global warming is astounding.

5. Noun clauses with *that* are used in reported speech. You use reported speech when you offer the opinions of experts in defending an argument.

   "The Kyoto Protocol is necessary to address the problem of global warming," said the world leader.

   The world leader said **that the Kyoto Protocol is necessary to address the problem of global warming.**

EXERCISE 10

Changing Quotes to Reported Speech with Noun Clauses

Use the sentences with quotes to form new sentences with noun clauses beginning with that. *The first one is done for you*

1. "There has been an overemphasis in this conference about drugs," said an AIDS adviser for Save the Children.

   An AIDS adviser for Save the Children said that there has been an overemphasis in this conference about drugs.

2. "There is no doubt that the Acme Company will be a difficult and even brutal competitor," company Chairman James Wilson said.

____

____

3. "The Justice Department's legal arguments and strategy were flawed," an airline spokesperson said in a statement issued after the Justice Department's announcement.

____

____

4. "When you are told you will be freed, you are filled with joy," said Colonel Ortiz.

____

____

5. "Without some encouraging news, the markets can't go up," said Johnson Investment's Bill Johnson.

____

____

If/Whether Noun Clauses

1. *If/whether* noun clauses begin with *if* or *whether.* Although both have the same meaning, *if* tends to be used in informal contexts and *whether* in more formal situations.

   The politician knows **whether/if she has enough money to run a campaign.**

2. *If* is generally used only when the noun clause is an object of a verb or follows an adjective. It is not used when the noun clause is a subject, a subject complement, or the object of a preposition. *Whether* can always be used.

   I wondered whether/if Alasdair might leave Scotland.

   I thought **about whether** Alasdair might leave Scotland. (object of preposition—*whether* only)

   The question is whether Alasdair might leave Scotland. (subject complement—*whether* only)

IMPORTANT NOTE:

Use statement word order in *if/whether* noun clauses.

I'm not sure **whether he is coming.**

Not: I'm not sure ~~whether is he coming.~~

EXERCISE 11

NOUN CLAUSES WITH *IF/WHETHER*

Use the questions to complete the sentences with noun clauses with if *or* whether. *Make only necessary changes. If both* if *and* whether *are possible, use* if. *The first one is done for you.*

1. Does she understand me?

   I often think about whether she understands me.

2. Could Kevin win the lottery?

   I wonder ______________________________

3. Would the seedlings grow in this soil?

   I'm not sure ______________________________

4. Would Valerie find customers in a new city?

   ______________________________ is the question.

5. Would I find friends who share my interests?

   I often think about ______________________________

EXERCISE 12

EDITING PRACTICE: GRAMMAR FOCUS AND SENTENCE CHECK APPLICATION

Read this paragraph carefully. Find and correct the seven errors in prepositional phrases and noun clauses. The first one is done for you.

An acquaintance of mine is a journalist who needed to take a trip to a rural area to take photographs for a story. He asked me to go along to assist him with carrying equipment, etc. I agreed to the amount of money he offered, but now believe that he ~~owed~~ owes me more money. He led me during the most primitive of places. That our living quarters did not even have running water or indoor plumbing I was surprised. For several hours in the day, I carried very heavy lights, cameras, and microphones. After we ate, I went to my room. Exhausted, I went to the bed without even using the well to wash. Later, I heard a noise that woke me up—it was a herd of sheep making noise. I was angry if they are so loud. I am not sure whether is he going to pay me extra, but I know that I deserve it for having to deal with the hard physical labor, the lack of modern plumbing, and the lack of sleep due to the sheep!

PART B

The Writing Process: Practice Writing an Argumentative Essay

Objectives	In Part B, you will:
Prewriting:	search for sources of information to support your argument
Planning:	practice categorizing and synthesizing information from outside sources
	use an outline to organize and sequence ideas for argumentation
Partner Feedback:	review classmates' outlines and analyze feedback
First Draft:	write an argumentative essay
	use "turning an argument on its head" as an introductory technique
Partner Feedback:	review classmates' essays and analyze feedback
Final Draft:	use feedback to write a final draft of your argumentative essay

The Writing Process: Writing Assignment

In the United States there is an ongoing debate about making English the official language of the country. While at first it may be difficult to understand the need for such a law, since more than 90 percent of the inhabitants of the United States have English as their native language, this has become a serious issue for many people on both sides of the debate. Your assignment is to write an essay arguing for one side or the other of this debate. You must justify your position with reasons that support your viewpoint. Follow the steps in the writing process in this section.

Prewriting: Searching for Information to Support Your Argument

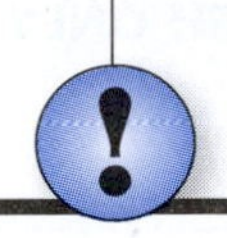

IMPORTANT NOTE:

Finding Relevant Sources of Information

When you search for information for your essay, follow these guidelines.

- Ask the reference librarians how to find the best sources for your topic. They can help you learn how to use electronic materials as well as find books and journal articles.
- Consider the sources carefully. Are the authors and publications credible? Is the article appearing in a well-respected and peer-reviewed journal? Again, a reference librarian can assist you in determining the academic quality of sources of information.
- Keep your notes carefully organized on note cards or typed in a word processing program.
- Make sure that you copy down all of the information you need to properly cite your sources, including the title, author, date of publication, journal title, publisher, page numbers, etc. See Appendix 5, pp. 247–249, as well as your style manual for more detailed information.

For an argumentative essay, prewriting usually involves actively seeking information about the issue. Although your teacher will tell you exactly how long or short this essay should be, it will be longer than the usual five- or six-paragraph essays you wrote for the assignments in other units. To develop your argument, you will pull together ideas from a number of different sources, including books, print journal articles, and Internet sources. Your teacher will give you specific guidelines about how many and which kinds of sources you need to include.

Ask a reference librarian at your school to assist you in finding relevant sources for your argumentative essay. Follow the guidelines in the Important Note as well as in Appendix 5, pp. 247–249, to begin gathering information about making English the official language of the United States.

Planning: Synthesizing Information and Using an Outline

Synthesizing Information

A synthesis is a combination of information from two or more sources. When you synthesize, you take information from different sources and blend them smoothly into your essay.

As you read about English only laws or "official English," you will notice that some of the same themes, for example, interference with human rights, reappear in more than one source of information. These themes and ideas will become the reasons you use to develop your argument. What are the themes and ideas that support both views that might be argued? List them.

ENGLISH ONLY LAWS—PRO	ENGLISH ONLY LAWS—CON
________________	________________
________________	________________
________________	________________
________________	________________
________________	________________
________________	________________
________________	________________
________________	________________
________________	________________
________________	________________

Review the information in the chart above. Which ideas do you agree with the most? Which column has more information? Choose one of the two points of view, for or against the issue; in other words, take your stance. Then write a tentative thesis statement that gives your position. Remember that an argumentative thesis statement is distinctive in that it takes a stand. You can change it later if you need to.

Tentative Thesis Statement: ________________________________

____

Categorizing Details

In your research, you will also notice that some sources of information offer more convincing details and examples than others to support the reasons in favor of or against English-only laws. These details and examples may take several different forms.

- A **definition of a key** term may help **explain a point.**
- To counter the opposing view, you might **compare and contrast** different approaches or beliefs about English-only laws.
- You might show a **cause-effect relationship** between one idea and another.
- You may also find **expert or scientific evidence** to support an argument.

To synthesize information from more than one source, you must choose only the best supporting details and methods of showing those details. For example, if you are arguing *against* English-only laws, one reason may be that these laws infringe on the rights of recent immigrants to a fair trial if it is in English and their language skills are not adequate to understand the proceedings. This is how the information might look in a chart.

Reasons	Details	Methods
1. *infringes on rights*	*may not get a fair trial*	*cause-effect*

IMPORTANT NOTE:

Remember that you will need to summarize and paraphrase information that you synthesize from sources. For information about these skills, as well as additional information about synthesizing, see Unit 8.

When you write your essay, you need to make sure that the methods make logical sense for giving the details that will support your argument. For example, you may want to use the definition method in your introduction section to provide background information about English-only laws. Later, you might want to quote an expert on this issue using the expert testimony method to provide supporting details for your argument. Be sure to keep careful notes about which sources you used for each of the details you add to your argument so you can cite your sources properly.

EXERCISE 13

COMPLETING A REASON/DETAIL CHART

For each ***reason*** *you find in your sources, write at least one* ***detail*** *to support it and a* ***method*** *of support for each side. Methods may include* definitions, explanations, comparison/contrast, cause/effect, *or* expert testimony. *You may need to add more rows to the charts.*

ENGLISH ONLY LAWS—PRO

Reasons	Details	Methods
1.		
2.		
3.		
4.		

ENGLISH ONLY LAWS—CON

Reasons	Details	Methods
1.		
2.		
3.		
4.		

Using an Outline

Writers usually develop argumentative essays using one of the three methods of organization discussed in Part A. Once you choose a method, you can create an outline that does two things: 1) states and supports your viewpoint and 2) states, acknowledges, and refutes the opposing viewpoint. Organizing the ideas that support your argument lends coherence to your argument, just as using transition expressions do.

Review the three methods of organization that you studied in the Methods of Organization section in Part A (p. 171).

EXERCISE 14

CREATING AN OUTLINE

Use one of the three methods of organization discussed in Part A (pp. x–x) to create an outline to develop your argument either in favor of, or opposed to, a federal English-only law in the United States. Using the information you collected on your research cards and in the chart in Exercise13, organize your outline on a separate piece of paper. You may want to refer to the patterns chart on p. 171 to help you.

Partner Feedback Form 1

Exchange outlines with another student. Read your partner's outline and answer the questions on Partner Feedback Form 1: Unit 7, p. 243, in Appendix 3. Discuss your partner's reactions to your outline. Make notes about any parts you need to change before you write your paper. For more information about giving partner feedback, see Appendix 2, p. 218, Guidelines for Partner Feedback.

First Draft

You are now ready to write the first draft of your essay. Before you begin, review your methods of presenting supporting details chart and any comments from your partner, especially the thesis statement suggestion.

EXERCISE 15

Writing the Introduction

Write an introduction for your essay, using your outline and the feedback you received from your partner. To begin your essay, use "turning an argument on its head" as explained on p. 17, Unit 1, and on this page. Both "Why Adopt a Vegetarian Diet?" on pp. 175–177 and "Coffee: Surprising Benefits from This Herbal Supplement" on pp. 179–180 use this introduction technique. You can use them as models if you want. End your introduction with a well-constructed thesis statement. When you finish, use the checklist to review your work.

IMPORTANT NOTE:

Turning an argument on its head means presenting the opposing view as a starting point. You can use this technique as a hook to generate interest and pull the reader into the essay. After you give the opposing view, you present your own view. Follow it with general ideas and background information about the issue at hand. Then finish your first paragraph with the thesis statement. Here are some tips for using this technique:

- Make sure that you can use the opposing view as a starting point in a way that makes sense logically. If you simply state both views, this is not "turning the argument on is head."
- Do not go into too much detail for this technique. Use only one or two sentences.

Examples:

Experts agree that developing nations should be encouraged to use modern agricultural techniques, purchasing equipment and seeds from large-scale Western agribusiness companies to bring them into the twenty-first century. However, the very practice of monoculture, or planting only one crop, destroys indigenous people's ability to produce food, shelter, and medicine for themselves.

When trying to finish a term paper or other homework, college students may need to drink caffeinated beverages or even take amphetamines to stay awake. Giving in to the urge to sleep however, by taking a short "cat nap," may in fact be just what you need to refresh yourself and be more productive.

Introduction Checklist

	YES	NO
► Did I effectively use an introductory technique such as turning the opposing argument on its head to hook my audience?	❑	❑
► Does my introduction include a clear statement of both sides of the issue?	❑	❑
► Do I take a stance with my thesis statement? Does my thesis statement provide a clear guide for the reader for the rest of the essay?	❑	❑

What is it? ______________________________

	YES	NO
► Are both views in the debate clear?	❑	❑

What are they? ______________________________

EXERCISE 16

Writing Body Paragraphs

Look again at your outline and at your introduction. Then complete the body paragraphs. Remember to use correct citation format for your researched information. When you finish, use the checklist to review your work.

Body Paragraph Checklist

	YES	NO
► Does each body paragraph treat only one main idea?	❑	❑
► Do I successfully follow the method of organization chosen for my outline?	❑	❑
► Does each paragraph contain a topic sentence with a clear controlling idea?	❑	❑
► Is my viewpoint on this issue clear to the reader?	❑	❑
► Do I successfully refute the opposing view?	❑	❑
► Are all my methods of presenting supporting details clear and effective? (Check the reasons/details chart in Exercise 13.)	❑	❑
► Does each paragraph end with a logical concluding sentence?	❑	❑
► Do my body paragraphs all relate to and support the thesis statement of the essay?	❑	❑
► Are my body paragraphs arranged in a logical order? That is, do they have coherence?	❑	❑
► Are all sentences in my body paragraphs relevant to the topic? That is, do they have unity?	❑	❑

EXERCISE 17

Writing a Conclusion

Review again your outline, introduction, and body. Write a conclusion for your essay. When you finish, use the checklist to review your work.

Conclusion Checklist

	YES	NO
▸ Does my conclusion successfully signal the end of my essay?	❑	❑
▸ Does my conclusion add coherence to the essay by:	❑	❑
a. restating the essay thesis?	❑	❑
b. summarizing or restating my viewpoint?	❑	❑
▸ Does my conclusion:		
a. leave the reader with my final thoughts on the stance I have taken on the issue?	❑	❑
b. make a prediction or suggestion about the topic of the essay?	❑	❑

Partner Feedback Form 2

Exchange essays with another student. Read your partner's essay and answer the questions on Partner Feedback Form 2: Unit 7, p. 245, in Appendix 3. Discuss your partner's reactions to your essay. Make notes about any parts you need to change before you write your second draft. For more information about giving partner feedback, see Appendix 2, p. 218, Guidelines for Partner Feedback.

Final Draft

Carefully revise your essay using all the feedback you have received: partner feedback, review of your outline and essay, instructor comments, and any evaluation you have done yourself. Use the checklist to do a final check of your essay. In addition, try reading your essay aloud. This can help you find awkward-sounding sentences and errors in punctuation. When you finish, add a title to your essay, and neatly type your final draft. See Appendix 4, p. 246, for information about writing titles.

Final Draft Checklist

	YES	NO
▸ Did I include a thesis statement that contains a clear topic and controlling idea?	❑	❑
▸ Which method of organization did I use to develop the argument? ______________		
Is the method clear?	❑	❑
▸ Did I argue for only one side of the issue? Did I adequately address opposing views?	❑	❑
▸ Did I synthesize information from different sources well? Did I use correct citation format?	❑	❑
▸ Did I use transition expressions correctly?	❑	❑
▸ Did I use prepositions and noun clauses correctly?	❑	❑
▸ Does each of my body paragraphs have a clear topic sentence?	❑	❑
▸ Does each of my body paragraphs treat one reason or subtopic to support the argument I make?	❑	❑
▸ Does my concluding paragraph successfully signal the end of my essay?	❑	❑
▸ Does my entire essay have unity and coherence?	❑	❑

Additional Writing Assignments from the Academic Disciplines

Beginning with the Prewriting activity on p. 191, use the writing process and write another essay. Choose a topic from the following list.

SUBJECT	*ESSAY WRITING TASK*
Business	Argue for or against moving a manufacturing plant to a less developed country than the United States. What are possible benefits to the host country? What might be harmful?
Science	Argue for or against accepting donations from pharmaceutical companies for scientific research.
Sociology/Political Science	Argue for or against accepting war refugees into more prosperous countries.
Linguistics	Argue for or against bilingual programs in public schools in the United States.

UNIT 8

Blueprints for

PARAPHRASING, SUMMARIZING, AND SYNTHESIZING IN ACADEMIC WRITING

Blueprints for Paraphrasing, Summarizing, and Synthesizing in Academic Writing

Objectives	In Unit 8, you will:
Analysis:	
Paraphrasing:	learn the difference between quoting and paraphrasing
	study paraphrasing examples
Summarizing:	learn summarizing guidelines
	study example summaries
Synthesizing:	learn the steps for synthesizing
	study synthesis examples
Practice:	practice paraphrasing and summarizing information
	practice synthesizing information while writing a cause/effect essay

What Are Paraphrasing, Summarizing, and Synthesizing?

In academic writing, you will often have to write about something you have read. Therefore, it is important to learn how to **paraphrase** (use different language to say the same thing), **summarize** (express the same idea in a smaller number of words), and **synthesize** (combine information from two or more sources) to answer a specific question of interest.

Study the diagram on the next page. It shows how you may paraphrase a source, summarize a source, and then use these skills to synthesize information from two or more sources into your original writing.

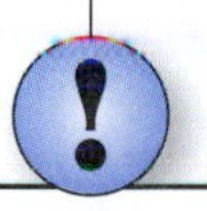

IMPORTANT NOTE:

Plagiarism is passing off someone else's writing and ideas as your own—like stealing what belongs to someone else. It is a serious issue in academic circles. If you turn in an assignment that you were supposed to write but did not write, you can suffer terrible consequences such as academic probation or even expulsion from a college or university.

Plagiarism is not always intentional. Sometimes you find information from a book, an article, or a web site that you believe is an excellent fact or support for your essay. However, if you do not put quotations around the exact words or paraphrase the information, you are in effect stealing the academic property of the original writer. In order to use source materials correctly and avoid plagiarism, learn the skills of paraphrasing, summarizing, and synthesizing and then apply correct documentation format. (See Appendix 5 for information about documenting sources.)

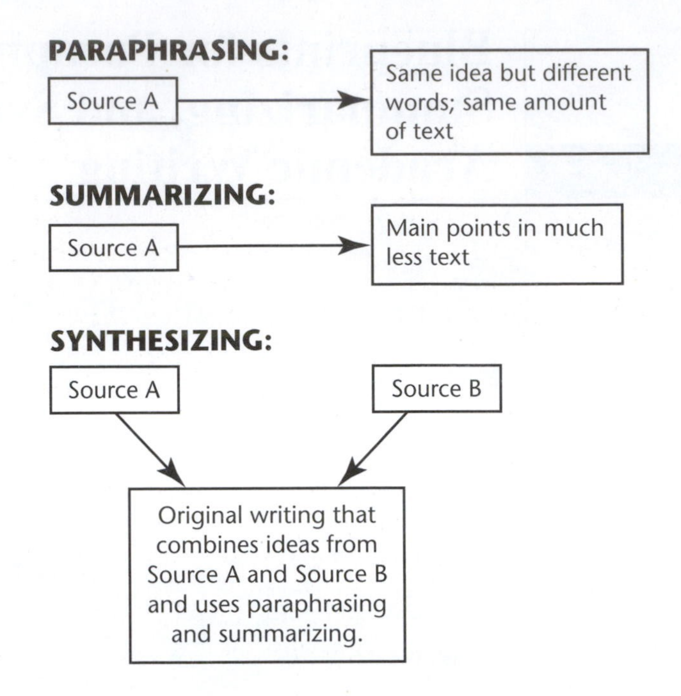

Paraphrasing

When you write an essay, you use your original ideas and information you have learned through experience. In addition, you often use information from print and electronic sources such as books, web sites, magazines, and newspapers. You can use such source information in two ways, and both ways show that you borrowed this information. The first way is to put *quotation marks* around the exact words.

Example:

According to a study in the *The Lancet,* "Lipid-lowering agents are known to reduce long-term mortality in patients with stable coronary disease or significant risk factors. Might they also be effective in reducing short-term mortality after acute coronary syndromes? An observational study suggests they are."

A second way of using information that is not yours is to **paraphrase,** or to re-state, another writer's words and ideas in your own words.

Paraphrase Example:

A recent study in *The Lancet* indicates that lipid-lowering drugs may increase short-term survival rates after acute coronary syndromes in the same way that they increase long-term survival rates for patients with stable coronary disease or with significant risk factors.

CAREFUL! In both of these examples, you need to avoid plagiarism and use parenthetical documentation to tell where you found the original material. (See Appendix 5 for information about documenting sources.)

IMPORTANT NOTE:

How do you introduce information from an outside source? One way is to use the phrase *According to* followed by the author's name or the name of the book.

Example: **According to** a report in the *New England Journal of Medicine*, . . . (your paraphrase)

Another way is to use the name of the source with a verb, such as *state, say, argue, believe, reveal, conclude, report,* or *suggest,* that indicates a sharing of the information.

Example: The *New England Journal of Medicine* **reported that** . . . (your paraphrase)

A good paraphrase conveys the same ideas and information as the original writing, but in different words. As the example above shows, the length of the paraphrase may be similar to the original, but the grammar and vocabulary are usually not the same. Key vocabulary, which may be technical, is often the same because there may not be another way to state it.

In English, the verbs that name a source (for example, *state, say, argue, believe, reveal, conclude, report,* and *suggest*) are sometimes used in the present tense rather than the past tense; however, both tenses have the same meaning.

Examples:

The New York Times **states** (stated) that tourism in New York City is at an all-time high.

The investigator **believes** (believed) that the ship's captain is responsible for the accident.

Examples of Paraphrasing

Paraphrasing is an extremely important skill for all academic writers. Study these examples of good and bad paraphrasing.

Original (13 words)

Selling a product successfully in another country often requires changes in the product.

Main idea to keep:

Companies must change their products to succeed in another country

Good paraphrase (15 words)

The most successful exporting companies have succeeded because they made important changes in their products.

1. *It keeps the idea that change is necessary.*
2. *Grammar is different* (*subject:* exporting companies; *verb:* have succeeded; *dependent clause:* because they made important changes in their products).
3. *Vocabulary is different* (successful exporting companies, have succeeded because, important).
4. *Length is similar to original.*

Poor paraphrase (14 words)

To sell a product successfully in another country, you need to change the product.

Main idea to keep:

1. The ideas are the same, but the wording is too similar (successfully, in another country). In fact, it is almost exactly the same. (Reread the original above.) This is plagiarism!
2. Though the length is similar to the original, only minor changes were made (Selling = To sell; often requires = you need to)

EXERCISE 1

Paraphrasing: Multiple Choice

*Read the original sentence. Then read the three possible paraphrases. Mark one **B** (Best), one **TS** (Too Similar), and one **D** (Different—or wrong—information).*

Pages 93–96

Unit 4—Blueprint Comparison/Contrast Essay 1: "Examining the Popularity of Julia Roberts' Characters"

1. *Despite the differences in these characters, perhaps it is their similarities that have attracted so many millions of moviegoers to **Pretty Woman** and **Erin Brockovich.***

_______ a. The main characters played by Julia Roberts in both *Pretty Woman* and *Erin Brockovich* were different yet possibly alike enough to draw many film patrons.

_______ b. Julia Roberts played Erin Brockovich and Vivian Ward, who were similar characters in two movies.

_______ c. Despite the distinction between these characters, one can draw a parallel that has attracted so many millions of moviegoers to *Pretty Woman* and *Erin Brockovich.*

SOURCE 2

Pages 66–68

Unit 3—Blueprint Process Essay 1: "Baby Talk"

2. *States of hunger, pain, or discomfort that cause crying and fussing are common at this stage.*

_______ a. Babies normally cry and protest during this phase because they hurt in some way or are hungry.

_______ b. States of hunger or discomfort that cause crying and fussing are frequent at this stage.

_______ c. States of hunger, pain, or discomfort that cause crying and protest are uncommon at this stage.

(continued)

(continued)

SOURCE 3
Pages 124–125

UNIT 5—BLUEPRINT CAUSE/EFFECT ESSAY 1: "MARKETING HEALTH AND FITNESS"

3. *Adolescents cannot escape the constant barrage of ads on television and radio and in magazines and newspapers. While some teenagers take this new-found knowledge and begin eating more appropriate foods and exercising regularly, others become obsessed with weight loss.*

_______ a. There is no escape for adolescents from the constant onslaught of ads on television and radio and in magazines and newspapers. Although some take this new knowledge and begin eating better foods and exercising regularly, others become fixated on weight loss.

_______ b. Even though there are many opportunities for teenagers to learn about proper diet and exercise, many disregard this information and focus solely on losing weight.

_______ c. Advertisements are constantly telling adolescents to be supermodel-thin; as a result, many teenagers starve themselves to death.

EXERCISE 2

PARAPHRASING PRACTICE: WRITE YOUR OWN

Read these original sentences and passages from Blueprint essays in other units. Circle what you consider to be the most important ideas. Then write your own paraphrase of the sentence or passage.

SOURCE 1
Pages 10–11

UNIT 1—"JOB SKILLS"

1. One way in which career counselors try to match people with their ideal jobs is according to the broadly-defined categories of skills that the jobs require.

Your paraphrase: ____

____

Pages 10–11

UNIT 1—"JOB SKILLS"

2. In fact, today's medical schools are giving almost as much weight to the interpersonal skills of their applicants as they do to their mental skills when evaluating these candidates for acceptance into their training programs.

Your paraphrase: ____

____

(continued)

(continued)

Pages 37–39

Unit 2—"Ten Thousand Teas"

3. The fresh tea leaves that are used for green tea are quickly steamed to halt bacterial and enzyme action common in fermentation.

Your paraphrase: ______________________________

____

Pages 37–39

Unit 2—"Ten Thousand Teas"

4. These two processes are repeated until the leaves become almost transparent and start to yellow or redden along the edges, which is a sign of the beginnings of fermentation.

Your paraphrase: ______________________________

____

Pages 97–98

Unit 4—Blueprint Comparison/Contrast Essay 2— "Two Kinds of English"

5. Pronunciation is perhaps the first difference that people notice between American and British English. Some individual sounds are consistently different. For example, PoTAYto in American English comes out as poTAHto in British English. WateR in American English is pronounced as wateH in British English. TUna in American English comes out as TYUna in British English. Furthermore, certain whole words are pronounced quite differently. *Schedule* is pronounced with a "k" sound in American English but with a "sh" sound, as *shedule,* in British English. The stress in the word *aluminum* in American English is on the second syllable, so it is pronounced aLUminum by Americans. Stress in this same word in British English is on the third syllable, so British English speakers pronounce it aluMInum. These pronunciation differences, though noticeable, do not impede real communication. In addition, neither American English nor British English has a better pronunciation than the other; they are simply different.

Your paraphrase: ______________________________

____

____

____

____

____

____

(continued)

Pages 175–177

(continued)

UNIT 7—BLUEPRINT ARGUMENTATIVE ESSAY 1—
"WHY ADOPT A VEGETARIAN DIET?"

6. One reason for becoming vegetarian is to prevent cruelty to animals. Animals, like humans, feel pain, stress, and fear. People cannot morally justify the pain and suffering of animals that are killed for food when adequate nutrition can be found in plant foods. Not only do animals experience these physical sensations when they are needlessly slaughtered for human consumption, but they are often treated cruelly prior to slaughter. Veal calves, for example, are forced to live in extremely small cages no longer than their bodies so they cannot move and create unwanted muscle. They are then killed when they are just twelve to sixteen weeks old so that their weak, immature muscles will produce soft meat.

Your paraphrase: ____

____

____

____

____

____

Summarizing

Remember that quoting and paraphrasing are techniques you can use to include information from another source in your writing. Another way to include information from another source is by **summarizing** it. A summary is a shortened version, in your own words, of someone else's ideas. These ideas may come from an article, a book, or a lecture. In college courses, knowing how to write summaries can be useful. For example, you may be asked to answer a test question with a short paragraph that summarizes the key points in your lecture notes. Before you can write a research paper, you will need to summarize the main ideas in your sources of information. When you summarize, you do not include all the information from the source. Instead, you use only the most important parts.

Summarizing involves not only writing but also reading and critical thinking. To summarize, you should do the following.

GUIDELINES FOR SUMMARIZING

1. Read the source material and understand it well.
2. Decide which parts of the source material are the most important.
3. Put the important parts in the same order they appear in the original.
4. Paraphrase (see pp. 202–207)— use different grammar and vocabulary. **You must write information in your own words.**
5. If the original states a point and then gives multiple examples, include a general statement with just one example.
6. Use verbs that indicate that you are summarizing information from a source (and not from your own head) such as *suggest, report, argue, tell, say, ask, question,* and *conclude.*

Remember that a summary is always shorter than the original writing. A ten-page article might become a few paragraphs in a summary. A two-hundred page book might become an essay.

Examples of Summarizing

Summarizing is a very important skill for a good writer. It is especially important when you are taking information from long sources. Study these examples of good and poor summarizing.

Original (190 words)

Selling a product successfully in another country often requires changes in the original product. Domino's Pizza offers mayonnaise and potato pizza in Tokyo and pickled ginger pizza in India. Heinz varies its ketchup recipe to satisfy the needs of specific markets. In Belgium and Holland, for example, the ketchup is not as sweet as it is in the United States. When Haagen-Dazs served up one of its most popular American flavors, Chocolate Chip Cookie Dough, to British customers, they left it sitting in supermarket freezers. What the premium ice-cream maker learned is that chocolate chip cookies are not popular in Great Britain, and children do not have a history of snatching raw dough from the bowl. For this reason, the company had to develop flavors that would sell in

Main ideas to keep:

1. Companies must change their products to succeed.
2. Examples of companies that did this: Domino's, Heinz, Haagen-Dazs, Frito-Lay.

Great Britain. Because dairy products are not part of Chinese diets, Frito-Lay took the cheese out of Chee-tos in China. Instead, the company sells Seafood Chee-tos. Without a doubt, these products were so successful in these foreign lands only because the company realized that it was wise to do market research and make fundamental changes in the products.

Main ideas to keep:

Good Summary (31 words):

Companies must adapt their products if they want to do well in foreign markets. Many well-known companies, including Domino's, Heinz, Haagen-Daz, and Frito-Lay, have altered their products and proved this point.

1. *It covers the main ideas.*
2. *It is a true summary, not an exact repeat of the specific examples.*
3. *It includes some new grammar, for example:*
   Original text: often requires changes
   Summary: modal is used: "companies must adapt"
4. *It includes some new vocabulary, for example:*
   Original text: Specific country names
   Summary: "many well-known companies"

Poor Summary (174 words)

Changes in a product are important if a company wants to sell it successfully in another country. For example, Domino's Pizza offers mayonnaise and potato pizza in Tokyo and pickled ginger pizza in India. In addition, Heinz has changed its ketchup recipe to satisfy the needs of specific markets. In Belgium and Holland the ketchup is less sweet. When Haagen-Dazs served up one of its most popular American flavors, Chocolate Chip Cookie Dough, to British customers, the British customers left it sitting in supermarket freezers. The luxury ice-cream maker learned that

1. *It is almost as long as the original and, therefore, not really a summary.*
2. *It includes almost the same vocabulary, for example:*
   Original text: the premium ice-cream maker
   Summary: the luxury ice-cream maker (This is plagiarism!)

chocolate chip cookies are not popular in Great Britain, and children do not take uncooked dough from the bowl. For this reason, the company developed flavors to sell in Great Britain. Since dairy products are not usually eaten in China, Frito-Lay removed the cheese from Chee-tos in China. In its place, the company has Seafood Chee-tos. Certainly, these items were so successful in these countries only because the company was smart enough to do market research and implement fundamental changes in the products.

Main idea to keep:
3. It includes almost the same grammar, for example:
Original text: For this reason, the company had to develop flavors that would sell in Great Britain.
Summary: For this reason, the company developed flavors to sell in Great Britain.
(This is plagiarism!)

EXERCISE 3

Summarizing: Identifying the Most Important Ideas

Reread Blueprint Process Essay 2 (Unit 3, pp. 70–71) "Exercise for Everyone." Choose at least four important facts and ideas from the essay. Then paraphrase each fact or idea in note form, using phrases, not complete sentences.

1. ______________________________

____

2. ______________________________

____

3. ______________________________

____

4. ______________________________

____

EXERCISE

Summarizing: Putting It in Your Own Words

Using your ideas from Exercise 3, write five to seven sentences that summarize the original message of "Exercise for Everyone."

____

____

____

____

____

____

Synthesizing

A synthesis is a combination of information from two or more sources. When you synthesize, you take information from different sources and blend them smoothly into your paragraph.

BASIC STEPS FOR SYNTHESIZING

1. Read the material from all the sources.
2. Choose the important ideas from each source. For this task, you must analyze the information. Ask yourself, "What is the author's purpose for writing this information?" Then decide which pieces of information are most important in accomplishing what the author intends. In synthesizing, it is always necessary to use only the important, relevant information.
3. Group together the ideas that are connected and that support each other.
4. Combine the ideas in each group into sentences, using your paraphrasing skills.
5. Organize the sentences into logical paragraphs and combine them into one continuous piece of writing. Be sure to include an introduction, well-constructed body paragraphs, and a conclusion. Do not forget to include any original ideas you have, too.
6. Check your work for accuracy and smoothness. Add transition words where they are needed.

Synthesis Examples

Synthesis is an important skill for academic writers who often use more than one source when writing papers. Study these examples of good and poor synthesizing.

Source A (81 words)

Switzerland is a great example of linguistic diversity because there are three different national languages. People in the central and northern areas speak German. People in the western area speak French. People in the southeastern area of the country speak Italian. Most Swiss can speak more than one language. One interesting fact is that the name of the country on its coins and stamps is not in any of these languages. Instead, "Helvetia," the Latin name for this country, is used.
Claudio Acevedo, Argentina

Main ideas to keep:
1. Geographical areas of Switzerland speak different languages.
2. Central and northern regions = German
3. Western part = French; southeastern region = Italian
4. The Latin name for Switzerland is used as well!!

Source B (68 words)

You might think that most people in Switzerland speak the same language because it is a rather small country. However, you would be wrong. Yes, the country is tiny, but there are four national languages. German is spoken by more people than any other language. The second most commonly spoken language is French, and Italian is third. A very small percentage of the people speak Romansch.
Najmuddin bin Faisal, Malaysia

1. Most Swiss speak German, then French, then Italian, and finally a few people in Switzerland speak Romansch.

Good synthesis (110 words)

Although Switzerland is a small country, several languages are spoken there. In fact, this tiny country has four national languages. The most commonly spoken language is German, which is used in the central and northern regions. The second most widely spoken language is French, which is used in the western area of the country. The third most-commonly used language is Italian, which is spoken in the southeastern area of Switzerland. A fourth language, Romansch, is spoken by only a very small percentage of the population. Ironically, the name for Switzerland on Swiss currency is not in any of these languages. Instead, *Helvetia,* the Latin term for this country, is used.

Main ideas to keep:

1. It has ideas from both sources (for example, Source A: German is spoken in central and northern regions; Source B: the most common language is German)
2. The ideas are woven together. (The most commonly spoken language is German, which is used in the central and northern regions.)
3. The sequence of the material is logical. (first, second, third, fourth most common languages)

Poor synthesis (88 words)

Switzerland is tiny, but there are four national languages. The languages in order of usage are: German, French, Italian, and Romansch. Portuguese and Greek are not spoken in this country. People in the western area speak French. People in the southeastern area of the country speak Italian. People in the central and northern areas speak German. One interesting fact is that the name of the country on its coins and stamps is not in any of these languages. Instead, *Helvetia,* the Latin name for this country, is used.

1. The ideas are not woven together very well. It is easy to see where one source ends and another begins. Source 2 information ends after The languages in order of usage are: German, French, Italian, and Romansch. Source 1 information takes up the rest of the paragraph.
2. The third sentence is an unrelated idea about Portuguese and Greek that is not from either source.
3. The sequence of the languages by geographical areas is illogical because it does not match the list of languages given at the beginning of the paragraph.

EXERCISE

SYNTHESIZING: ESSAY QUESTION PRACTICE

Imagine that you are a student in a sociology class. In an essay of five to eight paragraphs, write your answer to the essay question below using a word processing computer program. In your essay, synthesize information from a variety of sources.

SOCIOLOGY EXAM QUESTION

In a cause/effect essay, discuss the relationship between globalization and human rights. Briefly define globalization and human rights. Then explain how globalization has impacted human rights around the world.

Be sure to review the complete set of steps for process writing in the Part B sections of the previous units, including Prewriting, Planning, First Draft, Partner Feedback, and Final Draft. Pay attention especially to Unit 5 for information on cause/effect essays (See Unit 5, pp. 118–143.)

The following diagram will remind you of the synthesizing process. Although the diagram shows only two sources of information, ask your teacher how many sources you should use.

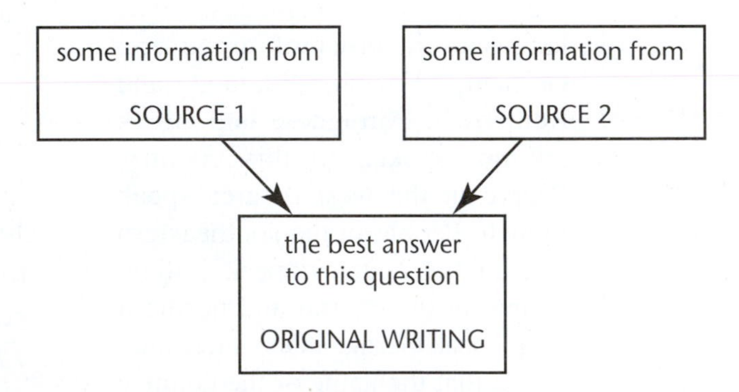

To develop your essay, follow these Basic Steps for Synthesizing.

Step 1: Read the material—Pull together ideas about globalization and human rights from a number of different sources, including books, print journal articles, and Internet sources. Ask a reference librarian at your school to assist you in finding relevant sources for your essay. **Remember to write down all the information you need about the sources to properly give credit.** (See Appendix 5, Finding and Documenting Information from Sources on pp. 247–250.)

Source 1: ____

____

Source 2: ______________________________

____

Source 3: ______________________________

____

Step 2: Choose the important ideas from each source—As you read about your topic in the sources, you will notice that some of the same themes reappear in more than one source of information. Decide which are the most important and relevant pieces of information and list them below.

Source 1: ______________________________

____

____

____

Source 2: ______________________________

____

____

____

Source 3: ______________________________

____

____

____

Step 3: Group together the ideas that are connected and that support each other—Place the ideas you listed in Step 2 into categories that fit together. Your list of ideas for each group may be longer or shorter than the lines provided.

Group 1 Main Idea ______________________________

Related Idea ______________________________

Related Idea ______________________________

Related Idea ______________________________

Related Idea ______________________________

Group 2 Main Idea ______________________________

Related Idea ______________________________

Related Idea ______________________________

Related Idea ______________________________

Related Idea ______________________________

Group 3 Main Idea ______________________________

Related Idea ______________________________

Related Idea ______________________________

Related Idea ______________________________

Related Idea ______________________________

Group 4 Main Idea ______________________________

Related Idea ______________________________

Related Idea ______________________________

Related Idea ______________________________

Related Idea ______________________________

Step 4: Combine the ideas in each group into sentences, using your paraphrasing skills—Using a word processing program, type the ideas you categorized in Step 3, combining the ideas in each of the groups into sentences.

Step 5: Organize the sentences into logical paragraphs and combine them into one continuous piece of writing, using transition expressions. Be sure to include an introduction, well-constructed body paragraphs, and a conclusion. Do not forget to include any original ideas you have, too—Revise and develop the sentences you created, organizing them coherently into an essay.

Step 6: Check your work for accuracy and smoothness. Add transition words where they are needed—Check your essay again for any revisions needed, and then turn it in to your teacher.

Paragraph Practice

Assignment: Write an original paragraph of 5–10 sentences about one of the following topics.

1. Your favorite writer or musician
2. The most difficult thing you have ever done
3. Advice for others who are learning the English language
4. Your dream house
5. The greatest invention of all time (in your opinion)

When you finish your paragraph, use the checklist to review your writing. If you answer "no" to any of the questions, revise your paragraph before you give it to your teacher for feedback and correction.

Paragraph Checklist

	YES	NO
▸ Does my paragraph have a clear topic sentence with a controlling idea that gives focus to the topic?	❑	❑
▸ Does my paragraph have unity? That is, do all of the sentences in it relate to the topic and develop the controlling idea?	❑	❑
▸ Does my paragraph have coherence?	❑	❑
a. Are the ideas arranged in a logical order?	❑	❑
b. Did I repeat key words, use appropriate pronouns, and/or use synonyms to make my ideas flow smoothly?	❑	❑
c. Did I use transition expressions to link ideas?	❑	❑
▸ Does my paragraph have a concluding sentence that relates to the ideas in the topic sentence and/or summarizes the ideas in the paragraph?	❑	❑

APPENDIX 2

Guidelines for Partner Feedback

Here are some guidelines about how to listen and talk to your partner about his or her work-in-progress:

- Begin by saying something positive about your partner's work, such as *The title really suits the essay* or *This is a great transition between paragraphs* or *You follow through well with the ideas in the thesis statement.*
- Be specific about what works well and what needs work. Avoid just saying *This is a problem* or *This part needs work.* Tell your partner **why** you think something needs work and specifically **how** you think your partner might fix it.
- Find a straightforward but polite way to suggest improvements to the writing. Avoid statements like *This is very bad* or *You don't make any sense.* Instead, use statements like *I found this part a bit confusing because . . .* , and *You might want to consider changing this part to include . . .* , and *I think this part might be more clear if you . . . .*
- When it is your turn to listen, take notes about how to revise your work based on your partner's feedback.
- Do not interrupt when your partner is talking. Try to save your response until he or she is finished speaking.

APPENDIX 3

Partner Feedback Forms

Partner Feedback Form 1: Unit 1 Paragraph to Essay

Writer: ____________________ Peer Reviewer: ____________________

Date: ____________________

1. Are the ideas in this outline arranged logically? ____________

   If not, what should be done to arrange them logically? ____________

   ____

2. Is there a thesis statement? ____________ If so, do the ideas in the body paragraphs support this thesis? ____________
   If there is no thesis statement yet, or if the thesis and the body paragraphs don't seem to work well together, what suggestions do you have for improvement? ____________

   ____

3. Does the introduction get your attention and make you want to read further? ____________ If not, suggest some hooks for the introduction here. ____________

4. How many body paragraphs do you think there will be in this essay?

   ____________ Will each body paragraph contain a clear topic sentence? If not, write possible topic sentences here.

   ____

5. Are the purposes of the conclusion clear? ____________ Do you think it will successfully signal the end of the essay? ____________

   Make any suggestions here. ____________

Partner Feedback Form 2: Unit 1 Paragraph to Essay

Writer: ______________________ Peer Reviewer: ______________________

Date: ______________________

1. What hook does the writer use in the introduction to this essay?

   ____

2. What is the thesis statement of this essay? Write it here.

   ____

3. How many subtopics are there? ______________ What are they?

   ____

4. Underline the controlling idea of each body paragraph in the essay.

   Does each body paragraph address a subtopic? ______________

5. Does the conclusion successfully signal the end of the essay?

   ____

6. What are the other purposes of the conclusion? Does it achieve these purposes?

   ____

7. Does each paragraph in the essay have unity and coherence? ______
   If not, what should be done to add unity and coherence to each paragraph?

   ____

8. Does the essay as a whole have unity and coherence? ______________
   If not, what should be done to add unity and coherence to the essay?

   ____

9. Were any parts of the essay not clear to you? ______________________
   If so, circle them on your partner's paper.

10. Do you think there is information missing from the essay? If so, what?

    ____

Partner Feedback Form 1: Unit 2 Classification Essays

Writer: ____________________ Peer Reviewer: ______________________

Date: ______________________

1. Are the ideas in this tree diagram arranged logically? ___________

   If not, what should be done to arrange them logically? ___________

   ____

2. Do all of the categories in the tree diagram follow the same principle of organization? _____________ Is so, what is it? _____________

   If not, what do you think it should be? ________________________

   ____

3. Is there a thesis statement? _____________ If so, will the ideas in the body paragraphs support this thesis? _____________ If there is no thesis statement yet, or if the thesis and the body paragraphs don't seem to work well together, what suggestions do you have for improvement? ____

   ____

4. How many body paragraphs do you think there will be in this essay?

   ____________________. Write a possible topic sentence for each body paragraph here. Share them with your partner.

   ____

   ____

   ____

   ____

Partner Feedback Form 2: Unit 2 Classification Essays

Writer: ______________________ Peer Reviewer: ______________________

Date: ______________________

1. What is the thesis of this essay? ______________________
2. How many categories does the writer include? ______________________

   What are they? ______________________
3. What is the principle of organization for the categories covered in the essay? ______________________
4. Does the introduction get your attention and make you want to read further? ________ If not, suggest some questions to use as hooks for the introduction. ______________________
5. How many body paragraphs are there? ________ Does each body paragraph contain a clear topic sentence? If not, write possible topic sentences here. ______________________
6. Is there a conclusion to this essay? ________ If so, are its purposes clear? ________ Does it successfully signal the end of the essay?

   ____
7. Does the writer use appropriate transition words, such as *one/another/a third (fourth, etc.)* + classifying word, for classification? Write them here. ______________________
8. Does the essay have any problems with unity and coherence? _____ If so, what? ______________________
9. Circle all the passives. Are they correct? ________ If not, suggest corrections here. ______________________
10. Are there any adjective clauses in the essay? ________ If so, are they formed correctly? ________ If not, suggest corrections here. ______________________

11. Are any parts of the essay not clear to you? ________ If so, circle those parts on your partner's paper. ________________________

12. Do you think there is information missing from the essay?

    If so, what? ____

Partner Feedback Form 1: Unit 3 Process Essays

Writer: ____________________ Peer Reviewer: ______________________

Date: ______________________

1. Are the ideas in the flow chart arranged chronologically? ________ If not, what should be done to arrange them chronologically?

   ____

   ____

   ____

2. Does the flow chart include all the details that a person should think about before, during, and after an oral presentation? Make suggestions here.

   ____

   ____

   ____

3. Are there any terms that need defining or sketches that should be included for the general audience who will be reading this essay?

   List them here. ______________________________________

4. Is there a thesis statement? ________ If so, will the ideas in the body paragraphs support this thesis? ________ If there is no thesis statement yet, or if the thesis and the body paragraphs don't seem to work well together, what suggestions do you have for improvement?

   ____

   ____

5. How many body paragraphs do you think there will be in this essay? ________ Write a possible topic sentence for each body paragraph here. Share them with your partner. __________________________

   ____

   ____

   ____

Partner Feedback Form 2: Unit 3 Process Essays

Writer: ____________________ Peer Reviewer: ____________________

Date: ____________________

1. What is the thesis of this essay? ____________________
2. Does the writer effectively use the funnel method in the introductory paragraph? ________ If not, what improvements can you suggest?

   ____

   ____
3. What process does the writer describe? ____________________

   How many steps are in this process? ____________________
4. Are the steps arranged chronologically? ________ If not, make suggestions. ____________________
5. Does the writer include enough steps so that a general audience could recreate this process (prepare and give a successful oral presentation)? ________ If not, suggest additional steps to include.

   ____
6. Are all unusual terms, such as the names of special equipment or tools, illustrated with sketches or defined in the essay? ________
   List here any unusual terms you think still need to be defined or illustrated for a general audience. ____________________

   ____
7. How many body paragraphs are there? ________ Does each body paragraph contain a clear topic sentence? If not, write possible topic sentences here. ____________________
8. Is there a conclusion to this essay? ________ If so, are its purposes clear? ________ Does it successfully signal the end of the essay?

   ____

9. Does the writer use appropriate transition words, such as *first* (*second, third,* etc.), *next, now, then,* and *finally; before, after, once, as soon as* and *while; during, over, between* + noun phrase, for process? ________________ Write the ones that the writer uses.

    ____

10. Circle all the articles in the essay. Are they used correctly?

    ________ Suggest corrections here. ________________________

    ____

11. Underline all adverb clauses in the essay. Label them according to what they tell: *why, when, where, how, for what purpose,* or *to introduce an opposite idea.* Are all of these clauses formed correctly? ________ If not, suggest corrections here. ________

    ____

12. Does the essay have any other problems with unity and coherence?

    ________ If so, what? ______________________________

    ____

13. Are any parts of the essay not clear to you? ______________
    If so, circle those parts on your partner's paper.

14. Do you think there is information missing from the essay? If so, what? ____

    ____

Partner Feedback Form 1: Unit 4 Comparison/Contrast Essays

Writer: ______________________ Peer Reviewer: ______________________

Date: ______________________

1. What two places (or topics) are being compared in this essay?

   ____

2. What do you think are the best three categories in the writer's T-Diagrams?

   ______________, ______________, ______________.

3. Can you think of any information to add under one of the T-diagrams? If so, add it to your partner's T-Diagram.

   ____

   ____

4. Are there additional subtopics for comparison/contrast that the writer did not include? If so, list some suggestions here.

   ____

5. Read the thesis statement. Does it indicate whether this is a comparison, contrast, or comparison/contrast essay? ______ If not, do you have any suggestions for rewriting the thesis statement to make this clearer? ______________________________

   ____

   ____

   ____

6. Based on the categories in the three T-diagrams, what will be the topic of each body paragraph?

   Body paragraph 1 ______________________________

   Body paragraph 2 ______________________________

   Body paragraph 3 ______________________________

Partner Feedback Form 2: Unit 4 Comparison/Contrast Essays

Writer: ______________________ Peer Reviewer: ______________________

Date: ______________________

1. What is the thesis of this essay? ______________________

   ____

2. How many subtopics does the writer include in this comparison/ contrast essay? What are they?

   ____

3. Is this essay mainly comparison, contrast, or both? ______________________

   ____

4. Does the quotation in the introduction get your attention? That is, does it make you want to read further? ______________________
   If not, suggest some quotations to use as hooks for the introduction.

   ____

5. How many body paragraphs are there? ______________________
   Does each body paragraph contain a clear topic sentence? If not, write possible topic sentences here. ______________________

   ____

6. Is there a conclusion to this essay? ______________________ Does it successfully signal the end of the essay?______________________

   If not, what suggestions do you have for improving it?

   ____

7. Does the writer use appropriate transition words for comparison/contrast? (*both* [noun] *and* [noun], *not only . . . but also . . . , nevertheless, on one hand . . . on the other hand, in contrast, whereas, unlike* + noun, *like* + noun, *conversely, although, even though, though*) Write some of the transition words the writer uses.

   ____

   ____

8. Does the essay have any problems with unity and coherence?

    ______________ If so, what are they? ______________

    ____

9. Were any parts of the essay not clear to you?______________
   If so, circle those parts on your partner's paper.
10. Do you think there is information missing from the essay? If so,

    what? ______________________________________

Partner Feedback Form 1: Unit 5 Cause/Effect Essays

Writer: ____________________ Peer Reviewer: ______________________

Date: ______________________

1. What career or field of study is the topic of the essay?

    ____

2. Based on the information in the chart, is this essay going to follow Method of Organization 1 (causes only), 2 (effects only), or 3 (causes and effects)?

    ____

3. Do all the causes and/or effects the writer has chosen seem logical?

    ____

    If not, why not? Make suggestions for changes. ________________

    ____

    ____

4. How many body paragraphs will the essay contain? __________

5. Read the supporting notes under the causes and/or effects listed. Can you think of other examples, explanations, or specific information to add? If yes, add it directly to your partner's chart.

    ____

    ____

6. After reviewing the chart, suggest a thesis statement that the writer might use.

    ____

    ____

    ____

Partner Feedback Form 2: Unit 5 Cause/Effect Essays

Writer: ______________________ Peer Reviewer: ______________________

Date: ______________________

1. What is the thesis of this essay? ______________________

   ____

2. What method of organization is used: 1 (causes only), 2 (effects only), or 3 (causes and effects)?

   ____

3. How many causes/effects does the writer include in the essay?

   ____

4. Is the introduction a dramatic statement? If not, can you suggest how to make the introduction more interesting?

   ____

   ____

5. How many body paragraphs are there? ______________________
   Does each body paragraph contain a clear topic sentence?

   ____

6. Are the supporting ideas for each cause or effect adequate? If not, suggest changes the writer might make to improve the support.

   ____

   ____

7. Does the writer use effective transition expressions? *(because/ as / since* + s + v; *therefore; consequently; thus; as a result* + s + v*/as a result of)* ______________________

8. Were there any parts of the essay that were not clear to you? ______________ If so, circle those parts on your partner's paper.

9. Do you think there is information missing from the essay? If so, what? ______________________

Partner Feedback Form 1: Unit 6 Reaction Essays

Writer: ____________________ Peer Reviewer: ______________________

Date: ______________________

1. Is there a thesis statement? ______________________ If not, what suggestions do you have for writing a clear thesis? ____________

   ____

   ____

2. How many body paragraphs will there be in this essay? ________
3. Will each body paragraph include relevant supporting details?

   ____

   If not, suggest details that may help support the emotion discussed.

   ____

   ____

4. Do you understand all the vocabulary in the chart? ____________

   If not, write the words you do not understand here. ____________

   ____

   ____

5. Do you think all the writer's ideas express an understandable and reasonable reaction to the photo? ____________________

   If not, make some suggestions for changes. ________________

   ____

   ____

Partner Feedback Form 2: Unit 6 Reaction Essays

Writer: ______________________ Peer Reviewer: ______________________

Date: ______________________

1. Does the introduction give an adequate description of the photo? ______________ If not, suggest a way to make the introduction more interesting. ______________________________

   ____

2. Is there a clear thesis statement? ______________________ If not, suggest a revision to make it more clear. ______________________

   ____

   ____

3. Does each body paragraph contain a clear topic sentence? ________ What is the controlling idea of each topic sentence?

   Topic Sentence 1: ____

   Topic Sentence 2: ____

   Topic Sentence 3: ____

4. In a few words, explain the general reactions of the writer in this essay. ____

5. Does the writer repeat key words or phrases in the essay? ________ If not, which key words or phrases do you suggest that the writer repeat? ____

   ____

6. Does the writer use pronouns to refer to previous nouns? ________ If not, suggest some appropriate pronouns and where to place them.

   ____

   ____

7. Does the writer use synonyms of common vocabulary to avoid sounding repetitive? ______ If not, can you suggest some synonyms of overly-used words? ______________________

   ____

8. Do the sentences have variety? (see pp. 157–158) ______ If not, how could the writer create sentence variety? ______________________

   ____

9. Were there any parts of the essay that were not clear to you? _____, circle those parts on your partner's paper.

10. Do you think there is information missing from the essay? If so, what? ______________________________________

    ____

    ____

Partner Feedback Form 1: Unit 7 Argumentative Essays

Writer: ______________________ Peer Reviewer: ________________________

Date: ________________________

1. Which method of organization did your partner use to outline the argument?

   ____

2. Was the method used successfully? _______________ If not, what can be done to correct it? ____

   ____

3. Is the opposing view stated? _______ Will it be refuted adequately?

   ____

4. Is there a thesis statement? _______ If so, will the ideas in the body paragraphs support this thesis? _______ If there is no thesis statement yet, or if the thesis and the body paragraphs don't seem to work well together, what suggestions do you have for improvement?

   ____

5. Do the ideas in this outline support the viewpoint of the argument? __________ If not, how can they be changed or worded differently?

   ____

6. Do all the details under each reason support the idea that they follow? _________ If not, explain here which ideas should be eliminated or expanded.

   ____

7. Do you think the writer has successfully synthesized information from different sources? ________ If not, make some suggestions for improvement. ____

Partner Feedback Form 2: Unit 7 Argumentative Essays

Writer: ________________ Peer Reviewer: ________________

Date: ________________

1. What is the thesis of this essay? ________________
2. How many reasons does the writer include in this essay to support his or her viewpoint? ________ What are they? ________

    ____
3. What is the opposing argument? ________________
4. Does the introduction get your attention? That is, does it make you want to read further? ________________ If not, suggest a way to **turn the opposing argument on its head** (or some other introductory technique) as a hook for the introduction here.

    ____
5. How many body paragraphs are there? ________________
Does each body paragraph contain a clear topic sentence?

    ____
6. Does the writer use appropriate transition words for arguments? *(although it may be true that/despite the fact that, certainly, and surely)* Write them here. ________________

    ____
7. Is the method of organization clear? ________________

    If not, how could the writer make it more clear? ________________

    ____
8. Is there a conclusion to this essay? ________ If so, are its purposes clear? ________ Does it successfully signal the end of the essay?________________
9. Were any parts of the essay not clear to you? ________ If so, circle those parts on your partner's paper.
10. Do you think there is information missing from the essay? If so, what? ________________

APPENDIX 4

Creating Essay Titles

When you write an essay for an assignment, you are usually required to include a title. Titles are not usually complete sentences. They are phrases that capture the essay's main idea or ideas and act as hooks to draw the reader in.

The main words in all titles are capitalized.
You should also capitalize:

- the first word
- the last word
- the first word after a colon indicating a subtitle
- the word after a hyphen in a compound word.

Do **not** capitalize:

- articles *(a, an, the)*
- conjunctions (*and, but, for,* etc.)
- prepositions (*on, of, between, under, through,* etc.)
- the *to* in an infinitive

Examples:

As You Like It

Writing Paragraphs: A Short Guide

Notes on the Observation of Drosophilae

The Tri-Petaled Flower

The How to Grow and Can It Book

Finding and Documenting Information from Sources

Finding Information from Different Sources

A research paper differs in at least two ways from the kinds of essays you have learned how to write in the early units of this book.

First, the research paper requires you to use information from more than one source of ideas. Also, as indicated in Unit 7, research papers are longer than an essay of five to seven paragraphs. To adequately develop your ideas about a topic, you must find out as much about it as you can to truly formulate your own thinking about it. You must take the responsibility for finding ideas beyond those given to you by your teacher in articles, handouts, or textbooks. You can find books, journal articles, and electronic materials at your college library.

Since the early 1990s, many libraries have begun to make electronic materials available. Students can now find electronic versions of print journals and newspapers. In addition to taking up less physical space in the library, these electronic materials are easier than print to search and find something specific.

In-Text Citations

When you include information from an original source in your final essay, you must cite this source in your text. There are several styles for citing material. One of the most common is to list the author of the material and the publication date.

In the examples that follow, note how the student writer uses part of Zumdahl's information in his work. Pay attention to the wording of the original source, the wording of the student writing, and the manner in which the information is cited.

ORIGINAL SOURCE

Although some chemical industries have been culprits in the past for fouling the earth's environment, that situation is rapidly changing. In fact, a quiet revolution is sweeping through chemistry from academic labs to Fortune 500 companies. Chemistry is going green. *Green chemistry* means minimizing hazardous wastes, substituting water and other environmentally friendlier substances for traditional organic solvents, and manufacturing productions out of recyclable materials.

From S. Zumdahl, *Introductory Chemistry,* (Boston: Houghton Mifflin, 2000).

Possible citation: According to Zumdahl (2000), green chemistry has three basic components.

Possible Citation: Zumdahl (2000) discusses the quiet revolution that is taking place within the chemistry world.

Student writing using the original source:

Most people would regard chemistry as a very traditional branch of science, but there are new hybrids of this traditional science. Green chemistry is a good example of a new version of a traditional field of study. According to Zumdahl (2000), green chemistry has three basic components, including creating fewer dangerous wastes, using water as a solvent, and working with schools to include tolerance. Because it is so new, green chemistry has yet to prove itself to be a true advancement over traditional chemistry. However, green chemistry seems to have a great deal of potential.

Common ways for writing the citation include:

- According to Zumdahl, this medicine has serious problems . . .
- Zumdahl found that this medicine had serious problems . . .
- Zumdahl reported that this medicine had serious problems . . .
- A report by Zumdahl showed that this medicine had serious problems . . .
- Zumdahl concluded that this medicine had serious problems . . .
- Based on Zumdahl's findings, we may conclude that . . .
- Based on Zumdahl's results, it may be concluded that . . .
- Because of Zumdahl's results, this medicine is no longer used . . .
- From Zumdahl's work, we know that this medicine has serious problems . . .
- Zumdahl proved that this medicine has serious problems . . .

IMPORTANT NOTE:

If your field has a special guide for citations, follow the rules or guidelines in that guide. Examples of special guides for citations include MLA (Modern Language Association), APA (American Psychological Association), and *The Chicago Manual of Style* (University of Chicago Press). In these guides, you will find examples for citing sources in the body of your essay; you will also find information about how to create lists of these sources at the end of your essay or research paper.

Reference Lists (Bibliographies)

In addition to citing sources, you will need to create a bibliography for these sources at the end of your paper. There are several styles for doing this. Here are some examples:

1. American Psychological Association (APA) Style—used for psychology, education and other social sciences
   a. For a book—Zinn, Howard. (1980). *A People's History of the United States.* New York: HarperCollins.
   b. For a journal article—St. Denis, V. (2000). Indigenous Peoples, Globalization, and Education: Making Connections. *Alberta Journal of Educational Research, 46*(1), 36–48.

2. Modern Language Association (MLA) Style—used for literature, arts and humanities
   a. For a book— Zinn, Howard. A People's History of the United States. New York: HarperCollins, 1980.
   b. For a journal article—St. Denis, Verna. "Indigenous Peoples, Globalization, and Education: Making Connections." Alberta Journal of Educational Research 46.1 (2000) 36–48.

3. Style Presented in *The Chicago Manual of Style*—used for most books, magazines, and newspapers of a journalistic nature.
   a. For a book—Zinn, Howard. 1980. *A People's History of the United States.* New York: HarperCollins.
   b. For a journal article—St. Denis, Verna. 2000. Indigenous Peoples, Globalization, and Education: Making Connection. *Alberta Journal of Educational Research* 46 (1): 36–48.

You should check with your teacher for the style he or she prefers that you use. In addition, the examples presented above illustrate only two common types of sources. For more information on how to include other types of sources (for example, sources written by more than one author, Web sources, etc), consult a publication style manual recommended by your teacher.

IMPORTANT NOTE:

Searching the Internet: The best way to find scholarly sources of information is through your college library. Doing a random Internet search for information for a research paper is not the best way to find credible, academic sources of information. However, you may want to search the Internet for information like the e-mail address of a professor who wrote an article you like, for example.

There are two primary ways to search for information on the Internet. One way is to use a search engine, like Google. The other way is to use a web directory like Yahoo. A good way to understand the difference between the two is to think of a search engine like an index in a book. It contains specific information about the entire book. A web directory is like the table of contents. It contains the broad categories that make up the chapters of the book. You would use a search engine when you are looking for something very specific, whereas you would use a web directory when you are looking for broader ideas.